The Graphic Syllabus
and the
Outcomes Map

The Graphic Syllabus and the Outcomes Map

Communicating Your Course

Linda B. Nilson

JOSSEY-BASS
A Wiley Imprint
www.josseybass.com

Published by Jossey-Bass
A Wiley Imprint
989 Market Street, San Francisco, CA 94103–1741   www.josseybass.com

Jossey-Bass books and products are available through most bookstores. To contact Jossey-Bass directly call our Customer Care Department within the U.S. at 800-956-7739, outside the U.S. at 317-572-3986, or fax 317-572-4002.

Jossey-Bass also publishes its books in a variety of electronic formats. Some content that appears in print may not be available in electronic books.

All sample syllabi used herein are reproduced with permission.

Composition: Lyn Rodger, Deerfoot Studios

Library of Congress Cataloging-in-Publication Data

Nilson, Linda Burzotta.
  The graphic syllabus and the outcomes map : communicating your course / Linda B. Nilson.
— 1st ed.
    p. cm.
  Includes bibliographical references and index.
  ISBN 978-0-470-18085-3 (cloth)
  1. Education, Higher—Curricula. 2. Curriculum planning—Methodology. 3. Graphic methods. I. Title.
  LB2361.N55 2007
  378.1'99—dc22
                              2007024540

Printed in the United States of America
FIRST EDITION
HB Printing 10 9 8 7 6 5 4 3 2 1

To my father,
Frank S. Burzotta,
who taught me the joys and benefits
of thinking visually.

About the Author

Linda B. Nilson is founding director of the Office of Teaching Effectiveness and Innovation at Clemson University, where she also teaches a graduate course in college teaching. She is the author of *Teaching at Its Best: A Research-Based Resource for College Instructors* (Anker, 2003), now in its second edition, and the co-editor of *Enhancing Learning with Laptops in the Classroom* (Jossey-Bass, 2005). She is presently serving as associate editor of volumes 25 and 26 of *To Improve the Academy,* the major annual publication of the Professional and Organizational Development Network in Higher Education (POD). (She will serve as editor of volumes 27 and 28.)

Over the years, Dr. Nilson has written many journal articles and book chapters and has conducted national and international sessions and workshops on dozens of topics related to teaching effectiveness, assessment, classroom management, and scholarly productivity.

Before coming to Clemson, Dr. Nilson directed the Center for Teaching at Vanderbilt University. Prior to this, she directed the Teaching Development Program at the University of California–Riverside (UCR) and taught a very popular graduate seminar on college teaching. At UCR she developed the "disciplinary cluster" approach to training teaching assistants, which received coverage in *The Chronicle of Higher Education,* and exported the approach to Vanderbilt.

Dr. Nilson entered the area of instructional and faculty development in the late 1970s while she was on the sociology faculty at UCLA. After she distinguished herself as an excellent instructor, her department selected her to establish and supervise its teaching assistant training program. As a sociologist, she published in the areas of occupations and work, social stratification, political sociology, and disaster behavior.

Dr. Nilson is active in several professional associations: on the regional level, the Southern Regional Faculty and Instructional Development Consortium; on the national level, the POD Network and Canada-based Society for Teaching and Learning in Higher Education; and on the international level, the annual Improving University Teaching Conference and the International Consortium for Educational Development.

A National Science Foundation Fellow, Dr. Nilson received her Ph.D. and M.S. degrees in sociology at the University of Wisconsin–Madison. She completed her undergraduate work in three years at the University of California–Berkeley, where she was elected to Phi Beta Kappa.

Preface

This book has been more than 25 years in the making. I first conceived of hand-drawing a flowchart of my course organization around 1980, but I didn't dare share the idea with a colleague. At the time, I was working at a Research I university, a place where faculty didn't talk about teaching and frankly didn't care what their colleagues did or didn't do in their classes. It took many years for the academic teaching ethos to start changing. Even in the early 1990s, it was still not completely acceptable for tenure-track faculty in research universities to discuss their teaching challenges or innovations. But in 1994, several years after I had started directing teaching centers, I finally sufficiently trusted someone with whom I could share my graphic syllabus idea. That person was Dr. A. Darlene Panvini, currently an associate professor of biology at Belmont University, who was then my assistant director of the Center for Teaching at Vanderbilt University. Not only did she instantly grasp the benefits of the graphic syllabus, but she went right to the task of designing one for her freshman seminar, Conservation Ecology. (Her creation is Figure 3.19 in this book.) She is the first person recognized in the Acknowledgments because her enthusiastic support gave me the courage to share the idea again and deepened my scholarly interest in visuals as teaching tools.

One reason to look to graphics to enhance student learning is that text, even though it remains the academic medium of choice, has had mixed success in motivating student interest and teaching concepts and relationships. Text worked quite well back when we used college as a social sifting and sorting mechanism; the students who survived were created in our image and knew how to learn from text. But text began to falter as soon as we started using college to educate the broader society. To add to the challenge, each successive student generation came to us having been raised with more and more captivating visual media, such as large-screen television, special-effects movies, surrealistic video games, and an increasingly animated web. By now, these media have supplanted the book as a major form of entertainment and as the predominant K–12 instructional tool. Chapter 1 in this book details the limitations of text in today's college population and argues for a change of media.

After I became interested in using graphics as teaching tools, I soon discovered that a cadre of psychologists trained in cognition and learning had already published a convincing body of research that supported the superiority of visuals for knowledge processing and memory. Chapter 2 summarizes this literature, making a strong case in favor of using visuals to enhance student learning.

If this work was so new to me, how familiar could it be to other faculty developers and faculty outside of psychology? Besides, haven't we Homo sapiens always depended more on our sight for survival than on any other sense? We certainly wouldn't have made it on our limited olfactory and auditory sensitivities, as most other mammals did. Perhaps our heavily literate culture will prove to be a short-term detour in the grander history of humankind.

Chapters 3 and 4 are largely devoted to showcasing model graphic syllabi and outcomes maps and recommending ways for you, the reader, to create these graphics yourself. Among the how-to suggestions on designing a graphic syllabus in Chapter 3 are five types of course organization that are relatively easy to represent visually, along with graphic syllabus examples. The how-to for an outcomes map simply extends the recommended way to design a course, which is around student learning objectives. A comprehensive list of objectives for a given course will include some that should be met early in the term, others to be met at various times in the middle, and the most complex ones to be achieved at the end. No doubt a few of the earlier objectives are designed to prepare students to tackle later ones. So why not sequence and flowchart all the objectives so students can see, in advance and as they progress, the process of their learning? Maybe then they will realize why they should bother to learn A, B, and C when all they are truly interested in is mastering X, Y, and Z.

Not surprisingly, these graphics enhance course organization, and Chapter 5 demonstrates how they uncover gaps, sequencing errors, tangential topics, and a general lack of flow in the ordering of course topics and learning objectives. A topical organization and a course design that are cohesive, logically constructed, and transparent *even to students* are likely to result in greater student learning, if for no other reason than that the students will find in these an accurate, ready-made structure for them to process, organize, and store the course material. Our minds retain only what they can file in a mental structure, and nothing provides structure like a memorable visual.

Appendix A features more than two dozen memorable graphic syllabi for an array of disciplines. The variety, creativity, and amount of knowledge available just for the looking are astounding. This is the most entertaining (and hopefully inspiring) part of the book. Information on affordable software for electronically creating graphic syllabi and outcomes maps is provided in Appendix B.

Reading this book requires that you engage both hemispheres of your brain. May you find it a refreshing and relaxing mental workout! If you are motivated to try your creative hand at a graphic syllabus or outcomes map, I would delight in your sharing the results with me.

Linda B. Nilson
Clemson, South Carolina
February 2007

Acknowledgments

It takes a village to write a book, even one that is single-authored. Some very generous and creative people have inhabited my village, and quite a few of them made meaningful contributions to the book. My gratitude goes first to Dr. A. Darlene Panvini, who was the first person with whom I shared the idea of the graphic syllabus while we both worked at the Center for Teaching at Vanderbilt University. She loved it and used it. Had she reacted tepidly, I would have put the idea back in the closet, where it had already spent 15 years, and there would be no book.

Thanks also to Dr. Patricia Connor-Greene, professor of psychology at Clemson University and the second person I confided in about the graphic syllabus idea. She was so encouraging that I got the nerve to start sharing it in workshops for the Clemson faculty and my colleagues at conferences. During one such workshop at the 2001 conference of the Society for Teaching and Learning in Higher Education in Newfoundland, I met Dr. Ernest Biktimirov, associate professor of finance at Brock University in Canada, who appreciated the graphic syllabus and other uses of visuals in teaching. We went on to coauthor three articles, disseminating our ideas in the field of finance. I thank him for being the finest possible collaborator.

Other individuals to whom I owe gratitude for their enthusiastic support are Dr. Cynthia Desrochers, my counterpart at California State University–Northridge, who so supported the graphic syllabus idea that she conducted workshops for her own faculty; Dr. Teresa Dawson and Dr. Martin Wall from the University of Victoria, who graciously went out of their way to collect graphic syllabi for me from their Canadian colleagues; Robert Littleson, lecturer in accountancy at Clemson, who wholeheartedly embraced the use of graphics in his teaching; Jennifer Russell at the Academy of Art University in San Francisco, who also provided contact help; and three dear colleagues—Dr. Kate Brinko at Appalachian State University, Dr. Andre Obérlé at the University of Scranton, and Dr. Barbara Millis at the University of Nevada–Reno—who invited me to facilitate graphic syllabus workshops with their faculty.

Over the years I was encouraged by many faculty and graduate students at Clemson and throughout the United States and Canada—and even a few from places as far away as Australia. Some of them shared with me their final graphic syllabi and outcomes maps and granted me permission to showcase them in this book. The graduate students in my fall 2006 College Teaching class—Irem Arsal, Uzay Damali, Pamela Galluch, Leslie Moreland, Samuel Otim, Mohammed Raja, Nicholas Roberts, and Jeff Shockley—submitted the highest quality graphics I had ever received from students in that course and gave me permission to display their fine work here. All of these creative people made this book possible and its graphics inspiring.

Special thanks are due to those who believed in the idea of my writing this book: Dr. Desrochers, Dr. Connor-Greene, and Mr. Littleson, who positively reviewed my book proposal, and Jim Anker, president of Anker Publishing, who nodded his approval with a book contract. My husband Greg supported my efforts every day, encouraging my writing, celebrating my progress with me, and never complaining about my longer work hours.

Finally, I thank my father, Frank S. Burzotta, to whom I have dedicated this book. A commercial artist with a deep appreciation for the visual arts, he taught me to draw as soon as I could control a crayon and started taking me to art museums when I was by far the youngest person in the building. He refined my artistic judgment and cultivated in me a visual way of thinking that I used throughout my schooling to help me understand and retain what I was learning in almost every discipline. This turned out to be a strategy well worth sharing.

1

The Limits of a Text Syllabus

By tradition, a syllabus is a text document. Over the years it has grown from a compact one- to two-page schedule of course topics, assignments, and tests to a five-page, ten-page, or longer laundry list of information required by institutions (e.g., Americans with Disabilities Act accommodations and academic integrity policies), some accrediting agencies (e.g., student learning objectives/outcomes), departments (e.g., number of office hours), and students themselves (e.g., policies regarding grading, attendance, tardiness, participation, late homework and papers, makeup tests, and the number of minutes to wait for a late instructor). The syllabus checklist shown in Figure 1.1 lists the *basic* information that should appear in a syllabus.

In response to the current litigious trend, some instructors have started putting a scheduling disclaimer at the end of the document. This provides them with some flexibility to adjust course activities to the students' background and progress and make allowances for illness, weather, power disruptions, and the like. Item #44 on the syllabus checklist provides the following legal caveat/disclaimer: "The above schedule, policies, procedures, and assignments in this course are subject to change in the event of extenuating circumstances, by mutual agreement, and/or to ensure better student learning."

In the same spirit, I recommend inserting an additional caveat/disclaimer after a list of student learning objectives/outcomes, as discussed in item #18 in the syllabus checklist:

> Students may vary in their competency levels on these abilities. You can expect to acquire these abilities only if you honor all course policies, attend classes regularly, complete all assigned work in good faith and on time, and meet all other course expectations of you as a student.

It is probably just a matter of time before some student initiates a lawsuit because, for whatever reason, he or she hasn't achieved the promised outcomes.

1

Figure 1.1

Syllabus Checklist

Basic Course Information

1. Course number, title, and credit hours

2. Classroom number and building

3. Days and hours of class meetings

4. URL of the course's web site

5. Required or recommended prerequisites, including permission of instructor

6. Breadth or major requirements the course fulfills

Section and Extra Sessions Information

7. Required or optional discussion sections or labs, with section/lab numbers

8. Name of teaching assistant

9. Classroom/lab room number and building

10. Days and hours

Information About Yourself

11. Your name and title (so students know how to address you)

12. Your office location, office phone, email address, and office hours

13. Your home phone and calling restrictions, such as "call before 10:00 p.m." (optional)

14. Relevant professional information about you, such as degrees and universities, teaching experience, research areas, other universities where you've worked, and relevant nonacademic experience

Information About Course Support Staff (teaching assistants, technicians)

15. For each staff member: office location, office phone, email address, and office hours

16. For each staff member: home phone and home phone restrictions (or have your teaching assistants develop their own syllabi)

Information About Course Coverage and Objectives

17. Course description, including "popular" topics the course does not cover

18. Your ultimate student learning objectives/outcomes—that is, what students will be able to do by the end of the course—as well as your major mediating objectives/outcomes. Add these caveats/disclaimers: "Students may vary in their competency levels on these abilities. You can expect to acquire these abilities only if

you honor all course policies, attend classes regularly, complete all assigned work in good faith and on time, and meet all other course expectations of you as a student."

Information on the Readings

19. Required and recommended books, articles, and the like with complete citations (author/editor, title, date, edition, publisher, journal, etc.), as well as price and where available

20. Existence of a course pack and where to purchase it

21. Why you chose the readings, at least the required ones

22. Where to find readings on reserve

23. Whether/where commercial lecture notes are available and how helpful they may be

Other Required Course Materials

24. Any required materials such as software, special calculators, cleaning supplies, safety equipment or clothes, art supplies, photography supplies, paper

25. Where to find/purchase them

26. Approximate costs

27. When they will be needed

Course Requirements and Grading Standards

28. Grading system (percentages, points, curve, etc.)

29. Graded course requirements:

   - How many of what types of assignments
   - Number and types of quizzes and examinations
   - Group component of individuals' grades, including peer evaluation procedures
   - Electronic communication
   - Class participation
   - Lab and discussion section assignments

30. General standards/rubric by which you will grade papers, problem solutions, other written work, electronic communication, and in-class participation (details come later)

31. Study and assignment aids to be distributed, such as study guides, review questions, directions for writing papers, lists of possible paper/project topics

32. Percentage of the course grade (and/or number of points) for each course component

33. Course requirements aside from those you compute in the grade. For example, "You will be expected to participate in discussion." "I will give unannounced, ungraded quizzes to see how well you are comprehending the readings and lectures." "In-class activities will include ungraded writing exercises and classroom assessment techniques."

34. Any extra credit options

35. Campus support services available to help students through the course, with their locations

Course Policies

36. How many minutes to wait for you if late

37. Policies on American with Disabilities Act accommodations

38. Policies on missed and late exams and assignments

39. Policies on attendance, tardiness, class participation, and classroom decorum

40. Policies on academic integrity, including in collaborative work

41. Policies and procedures on lab safety and health, if applicable

Course Organization and Schedule

42. Overall course organization/"flow" and your rationale for it

43. Class-by-class or weekly schedule, preferably in grid format or with an alternative graphic representation (e.g., graphic organizer) attached. Provide as much of the following information as possible:

    • Substantive topic(s)

    • Readings, papers, or other homework assignments due for each class

    • In-class activities and formats (e.g., lecture, group meetings, class discussion, role-playing, simulation, debate, student presentations, case studies, field trips, film, video, slide show, visiting speaker, review session, exam, announced quiz)

44. Legal caveat/disclaimer: "The above schedule, policies, procedures, and assignments in this course are subject to change in the event of extenuating circumstances, by mutual agreement, and/or to ensure better student learning."

Grunert (1997) proposes a learning-centered syllabus that incorporates considerably more information than the syllabus checklist recommends: instructions on how to use the syllabus; a letter of reassurance to the students, especially if they look on the subject matter as particularly challenging; a discussion of the purpose of the course; a list of the learning objectives for each course unit as well as the entire course; a guide to the readings; detailed instructions for all homework and other assignments; detailed criteria for the grading of these assignments; the procedures the instructor will follow for dividing students into teams; information on the test questions; a learning styles inventory; recommendations on how to study for the course, along with learning tools and aids; and course content information. In her view, a syllabus should be a course manual that serves many purposes—as many as 16—including acquainting students with the instructor's approach to education, the nature of active learning, good note-taking strategies, and a variety of learning resources.

The Skeletal Structure of a Course

The backbone of a course—and therefore, of the syllabus—comprises only two things: the organization and schedule of topics the course addresses and the list of student learning objectives/outcomes. The former has been an essential component of the syllabus for decades, and the latter has become essential over the past 10 or so years to meet accountability and accreditation requirements. Outside demands aside, both components together provide the skeletal structure of a course. The topical organization and schedule lay out the content the course will contain and how that content will be chunked and ordered, while the student learning objectives/outcomes map out what student will learn to *do* with the content—that is, the skills and abilities that students should acquire during the course. The outcomes should also dictate the criteria on which students will be assessed and graded and, at the very least, inform the predominant teaching methods, the in-class and out-of-class activities, and the type of assignments. After all, the whole purpose of the methods, activities, and assignments are, or should be, to prepare students to achieve those objectives/outcomes, and some of these are more effective than others at helping students learn various skills (Fink, 2003; Goodson, 2005; Nilson, 2003).

To expand on this last point, research tells us that lecture alone is a poor tool for enabling most students to meet most objectives/outcomes. While some instructor modeling has its place, listening to lectures, even when good notes are taken, will not help students learn to think critically about the subject matter, to write or speak well, to solve problems, to think critically, to transfer knowledge to new situations, to make ethical decisions, to perform techniques or procedures, to practice an art form, or to create *anything*. And only rarely will lectures impact their attitudes, values, and beliefs about the subject matter (Bligh, 2000; Bonwell & Eison, 1991).

However, integrating appropriate class activities every 10 to 20 minutes during the lecture can greatly increase students' comprehension and retention of that material (Crouch & Mazur, 2001; Rowe, 1980; Ruhl, Hughes, & Schloss, 1987). Depending on the activity, they can give the students practice in any type of cognitive operation (Goodson, 2005). Pausing a lecture for students to solve a problem helps them develop application skills and problem-solving strategies. Having them answer, discuss, then re-answer a conceptual multiple-choice item gives them the chance to analyze and abstract what they just heard, as well as to evaluate their understanding of the material (Crouch & Mazur, 2001). Giving them 5 to 10 minutes to debrief a mini-case using the principles just explained affords them practice in situational analysis, problem definition, application, and evaluation of alternative interpretations and solutions.

These examples illustrate small teaching "moves" that serve well as student-active lecture breaks. Beyond the interactive lecture, there are other major teaching methods that provide students with learning experiences that develop a range of relatively advanced cognitive and affective abilities. Problem-based learning, for example, fosters skills in fuzzy-problem analysis, research, information literacy, data synthesis, evaluation of alternatives, and collaboration, as well as tolerance for ambiguity and uncertainty. Simulations and games help students achieve outcomes such as situational analysis, extrapolation and forecasting, risk-and-reward assessment, and strategy development, which combine into a sophisticated type of application. When closely connected to course goals, content, and in-class activities, service-learning helps students meet other objectives/outcomes, some of them affective, such as acquiring a more accurate understanding of social problems, thinking more critically, developing empathy with diverse people, honing leadership and other life skills, and enhancing a sense of civic and social responsibility (Eyler & Giles, 1999; Gray, Ondaatje, Fricker, & Geschwind, 2000).

Of course, instructors can usually choose among several teaching methods and moves to accomplish the same objective. The requirement is that there be a close *correspondence* among learning outcomes, the learning experiences that help students achieve them, and the means of assessment. The learning experiences, such as in-class and out-of-class activities, should give students practice in performing whatever mental or physical actions the objectives describe, which in turn should be mirrored in the assignments and tests that serve as formal assessments.

The Syllabus as Scholarship

It is no coincidence that no two syllabi look alike, even for the same course. A syllabus reflects the professional judgment of faculty in higher education, a group of individuals who are notorious for forging their own pathway. What instructor with any classroom experience prefers to be handed a syllabus to teach from that has been developed by a committee or colleague? We tend to believe that a syllabus should be a *personal* creation that reflects one's intellectual viewpoint on the subject matter. So instructors spend hours, even days, designing a course and its syllabus, as well as poring through books for the syllabi that most closely mirror their preferred organization and slant on the material.

In a deep sense, a syllabus is a piece of scholarship, one that brings the scholarship of integration to the scholarship of teaching (Boyer, 1990). For any given course, your syllabi display your conception of how a field or subfield is organized—or *should* be organized for the purpose of communicating it—and how students can best master its knowledge and skills. Your teaching philosophy is readable between the lines of your syllabus, as well as in parts of the text itself. The document, especially your assignments and class-time plans, is a window to your theories of teaching and learning, whether you see yourself as a knowledge transmitter, a resource, a facilitator, a manager, an experience creator, or an activist.

If a syllabus contains enough detail, it can show how "honest" an instructor is in assessing his or her students. Instructors who claim their courses will help develop higher order thinking skills, but who assess students using testbank multiple-choice items, are not being totally honest with the students, and probably not with themselves.

Colleges and universities that evaluate teaching effectiveness using anything that even resembles a teaching portfolio require faculty to submit the most recent syllabus they have used for each course. While we may not talk about it, we know a syllabus reveals a lot about our colleagues. By the "warmth" of the language and the strictness of certain course policies, it conveys how approachable and flexible they want to appear to their students. By the degree of organization and detail in the schedule of topics and assignments, a syllabus gives an indication of how well they plan ahead and, more generally, how much they like structure. The presence or absence of assignments and activities that hold students accountable for the readings sheds light on whether the instructor lectures the readings in class, or doesn't focus on the readings, or is simply naive to students' study habits.

The types of assignments and tests that colleagues give provide reality-checks on their stated student learning objectives. In order to develop genuinely high-order cognitive and affective abilities, students must typically do considerable reflection, writing, and sometimes out-of-class research. Objective quizzes and tests are seldom up to the task. More "personal" and student-choice assignments suggest that the instructor is interested in his or her students' development as whole persons.

A syllabus can reveal aspects of an instructor's teaching philosophy, methodological preferences, and educational politics. Key terms such as *empowerment* (as applied to the student) and *learner-centered* say one thing, while *lecture, transmission,* and many internal-state verbs among the outcomes (student will *know, learn, understand*) hint at the opposite way of thinking.

Where the Text Syllabus Fails

We know very little about how students respond to syllabi. We don't really know what kind of information they home in on to decide whether to stay in or drop a course. We don't really know if they "size us up" by interpreting certain words, the tone, course policies, and information on tests, assignments, and activities the same way our colleagues do. With a bit of research to draw from, we can surmise that the savvy students at least examine the amount of out-of-class work (readings and assignments) and the testing schedule to determine whether they can "manage" their way through the semester while carrying the course (Nathan, 2005).

The only thing we *do* know about how students respond to syllabi is that many students don't read them carefully or completely. We know this from our own experience, of course—largely from the many questions we get from students throughout the semester that were answered in the syllabus—and from teaching tips we occasionally learn about that induce students to read the syllabus (Nilson, 2003). One such tip is to have each student sign a contract stating that he or she has read the syllabus and understands its contents, including course grading, attendance policies, and the institution's grading policies (T. I. D. Campbell, personal communication, September 27, 2001). Another tip is to break students into groups and have them scavenger-hunt important pieces of information in the syllabus. (Bring some goodies with you to reward the fastest and most accurate team.) Or give students a test on the syllabus on the second day of class, and have it count toward the final grade. Not all the questions need be simple facts from the syllabus, such as the number of tests, the point value of various assignments, and the authors of the major readings. You can also ask questions that obtain useful information about your students, such as the learning objectives they are most anxious about meeting and the course topics of greatest interest to them (Nilson, 2003).

But why do we have to goad students into reading the syllabus carefully? All syllabi contain standard information of the type students seem to want to know (e.g., test dates, assignment due dates, the attendance policy, what happens to work submitted late), yet many students don't consult them. Because these documents are typically posted on the web, students can't actually "lose" them. Why don't all students refer to their syllabus for what they want to know?

Could the reason lie in the fact that the syllabus is all text? As we will see in the next chapter, today's younger students comprise a visually oriented generation. They are not on the friendliest of terms with the printed word—at least not with *pages* of printed words. Only half of 18- to 24-year-olds in the United States read a book of *any* kind in 2002, and only 22% of 17-year-olds read daily in 2004, a drop from 31% in 1994 (Hallett, 2005). The average reading speed for college students hovers around an unimpressive 250 words per minute and only 100 words per minute for scientific and technical material (Soleil, 2003)—the rate is slower for first-year students, faster for seniors. And many students cannot focus their minds on academic material for more than five minutes (Blue, 2002). It's no wonder they dread tackling their reading assignments, and the vast majority don't do them without sufficient sanctions and/or rewards (Burchfield & Sappinton, 2000; Hobson, 2004; Marshall, 1974; McDougall & Cordiero, 1993; Nathan, 2005; Self, 1987). Why should the ever-lengthening text syllabus be any different?

Even if students do read the syllabus, the content-heavy sections might not make much sense to them. Certainly one of the most content-laden sections is the schedule of topics that the course addresses. The topics usually contain technical terms of the discipline, terms with which the students are initially not familiar. If they already knew these terms, they wouldn't be in the course to learn about them. Not surprisingly, the topics in syllabi in the sciences, mathematics, and engineering are almost exclusively technical words that a typical student wouldn't understand until well into the course.

Even courses in nontechnical disciplines use a technical vocabulary. The following list of topics is from a cross-disciplinary freshman seminar called "Free Will and Determinism" that I taught a few years ago:

- Modern philosophical perspectives on free will and determinism

- Compatibilism

- Fatalism

- Modern genetic, biochemical, and sociobiological evidence for determinism

- Historical materialist determinism of the late 19th century

- The specter of programmed sociopolitical determinism in the 1930s

- The utopian possibilities of programmed determinism: Behaviorist psychology of the mid-20th century

- Latter 20th-century sociology: Symbolic interactionist school

- Latter 20th-century sociology: Conflict theory (political sociology)

- Clinical psychology's self-help therapy of the 1970s and 1980s

- The new age psycho-spiritual perspective of the late 20th century

No doubt all the students came into my course knowing the nontechnical meanings of free will and determinism, or they would not have selected that seminar from the dozens available. They were also familiar with the time periods in the topic list. Most students probably had a working understanding of the terms *fatalism, genetic,* and *biochemical,* and for some, the phrase *clinical psychology* as well. But how many first-year students would correctly comprehend the concepts of compatibilism, sociobiological, historical materialist, sociopolitical, utopian, programmed (in the psychological sense), sociology, symbolic interactionist, conflict theory, and new age?

If the students don't know what most (or any) of the topics mean, what are the chances that they will be able to perceive the organization of the course? A sense of organization is based on an understanding of the concepts and terms being organized. No one can grasp the organization of nonsense words unless the arrangement is alphabetical, which in itself has no relation to content.

Figure 1.2 provides a whimsical example of how students might perceive a syllabus in an area they know (and care) little about. While the words look familiar, they also seem foreign because they make no sense in their context. As far as the students are concerned, there *is* no context. They don't see the relationship between the composition of apple peel and giraffe consciousness, though they may figure that these coming so early in the semester furnish a foundation for the course content. In fact, they don't see *any* relationships among the topics. Certainly they can pick up on the repetition of words. They can see that the course will address two aspects or parts of the modern car and will return to giraffe consciousness at a more advance level just after mid-semester. But these trivial insights don't give them a clue as to the overall organization of the course or its subject matter.

Figure 1.2

How Students Might See a Syllabus

Organization of Course BLAH 300: "Something I Gotta Take"

Week 1: Overview of Something I Gotta Take

Week 2: The Composition of Apple Peel

Week 3: Introduction to Giraffe Consciousness

Week 4: Cooking with Sugar and Eggs

Week 5: Sugar and Eggs Continued: Challenges and Solutions

Week 6: The Modern Car: The Carburetor

Week 7: The Modern Car: Seat Belts

Week 8: Advanced Giraffe Consciousness and Introduction to Pineapples

Week 9: The Relationship Between Pineapples and Buses

Organization itself might not be so critical if the mind weren't so dependent on it for deep learning and memory. We process, recall, and retrieve knowledge not as a disparate aggregate of factoids but as an interrelated structure, a coherent whole with interconnected parts. In fact, learning and storage take place *only* in the context of a logically organized conceptual framework. Deep processing, as opposed to simple memorization, necessitates seeing the structure of new knowledge and integrating it into one's existing structure of prior knowledge (Anderson, 1984; Bransford, Brown, & Cocking, 1999; Rhem, 1995; Svinicki, 2004).

The organization of knowledge originates in the mind's perception of patterns and relationships across observations. Identifying patterns and connections is one of the mind's most important jobs. Through this process the mind devises logical foundations for *generalizing* from observations and *simplifying* reality. Otherwise, we would find reality too complex to operate within. We would experience repetitive events as novel every time they occurred, and we'd learn and remember nothing from them. The human mind is not unique in this capacity. Except where instincts are involved, animals learn the same way—or so suggest countless behaviorist experiments on the operant conditioning of mice, rats, pigeon, dogs, and chimpanzees.

Our thinking is so dependent on structure that if we don't have an established, complete logical structure to interpret and explain an observed phenomenon, we will *make up* connecting pieces or entire theories. For instance,

Charles Darwin could not have observed mutations in progress, but he hypothesized, apparently correctly, that they do occur and are responsible for species diversity. However, making up connections is risky business and we may be wrong. The now-classic videotape produced by Harvard University, *A Private Universe,* dramatically shows that many intelligent people will spin their own incorrect theories about common phenomena, such as the causes of the seasons, if they have not heard and deep-processed the scientific explanation. And once a human mind adopts a certain explanatory structure, it won't easily let go of it. The mind demands a lot of reteaching and convincing that the new explanatory structure is superior to its own self-generated invention.

Let's bring all this cognitive psychology back to our students. They are disciplinary novices, and as such, they tend to miss the patterns and structures that we experts recognize so easily. Of course, we have internalized the most accurate explanatory structure and have stored a vast amount of knowledge and terminology within it. Students may come to our classes with faulty models and assorted misconceptions, and they definitely arrive without much prior knowledge and disciplinary vocabulary. Lest they leave our classes unchanged, we have much more to share with them than a lump of new content and the things they can do with that content. We must provide students with discipline-related structures in which to understand and retain the course content—that is, an appropriate organization of the new knowledge, and strategies to help students reconcile and integrate that knowledge with the structure of understanding they currently have (e.g., practice in reinterpreting their prior observations and experience).

Those in need of the most structure to guide their learning are students with little or no prior knowledge of the subject matter. Those with a sound content background should already have a viable structure to impose on new knowledge and to facilitate its integration with their prior knowledge (Anderson, 1984; Bransford et al., 1999; Svinicki, 2004). But it is difficult to judge the course level at which students may acquire a strong enough background, and this no doubt varies across individual students.

How should we supply this structure in our courses? Not with more text. With the current generation of students, we are likely to communicate more effectively using the "language" of graphics. There are two graphic tools that are useful for conveying the structure of our subject matter and what we expect our students to be able to do with it.

The first of these tools is the graphic syllabus, which is a flowchart of the organization and schedule of course topics. This essentially is a visual depiction of the instructor's conception of the organization of a field or subfield for the purpose of communicating it to students. It is as much a piece of scholarship as the text syllabus.

The second graphic tool is the outcomes map, a flowchart of the expected, sequenced progression of students from the early-in-the-course learning objectives, through the during-the-course mediating objectives, to the end-of-the-course ultimate objectives. To be logically cohesive, a course should be designed on the principle that meeting earlier objectives prepares students to meet later objectives. With an outcomes map, students can see exactly how their knowledge and skills will progress through the course and gain a sense of the criteria on which they will be assessed during the course.

This does not mean that we should abandon the text syllabus. The text syllabus allows us to provide a level of detail that might not be achievable in a graphic syllabus due to space limitations. These graphic tools are meant to complement and supplement the text syllabus.

Visuals communicate the structure of and interrelationship among the topics to be covered and the abilities students will acquire. As we will see later, they can also be designed to communicate an instructor's approachability, sense of humor, and caring for the students. But why use *graphics* to communicate? The next chapter reviews the literature on their pedagogical power, which the academy has underappreciated until now.

2

How and Why
Graphics Enhance Learning

We humans have always been visual animals—though perhaps by default. After all, we lack the olfactory sentience of most other mammals and the auditory range and sensitivity of many of them. But our eyes serve us well. They can differentiate colors, shapes, and distances rather well for a mammal, even if they could never compete against those of an eagle. We relied on them more than on any other sense for virtually all our early survival activities: hunting, fishing, gathering, making fire and tools, distinguishing the edible from the poisonous, identifying and dodging predators, planting and harvesting, and "reading the sky" for the time of day and time of year. And we survived rather well—well enough to have the time to paint the walls of our caves. Chances are that we developed visually oriented early civilizations before we refined language into a universally useful formal tool and made music into a captivating art form.

Maybe we haven't relied quite as much on our eyes the past few millennia, during which more oral cultures, then literate ones, have proliferated. Even then, we use our eyes to read. But we seem to be coming full circle. Over the past several years, we have seen a reemergence of a more visual culture, one in which knowledge and information are *increasingly* conveyed in graphical forms and are *decreasingly* communicated in text (Fischman, 2001; Hartman, 2006). Raised on television, movies, video games, and the Internet, today's young people are leading this cultural shift. It is little wonder that traditional-age students find distance education and computer-assisted instruction so appealing. These educational venues depend on graphical presentations of course material, along with interactivity, for their success (Cyrs, 1997). Those in the instructional and information technology industries project that visually based, interactive learning will proliferate and soon dominate the educational media.

> Visualization will be at the heart of knowledge and under-
> standing in the coming decades. In a world characterized by
> increasingly complex information sets, our ability to acquire
> and understand them quickly will become central to effec-
> tive performance. As visualization technologies evolve, we
> can expect to see the spoken and written word, our domi-
> nant modes of sharing today, eclipsed in many instances by
> 3-dimensional, highly interactive and compelling models,
> simulations, and augmented realities. (Hodgins, 2000, p. 9)

A great deal of all sensory learning is visual and always has been, but only
recently have educators started paying attention to this fact and launched a visual literacy movement (Avgerinou & Ericson, 1997). The use of visuals—
flowcharts, concept maps, mind maps, thinking maps, diagrams, charts,
graphs, and pictures—is catching on in the educational world at all levels, especially for interpreting and supplementing challenging print material. No
doubt the spread of online and hybrid learning environments has helped this
movement. In fact, a large body of research documents that graphics of all
kinds are powerful teaching and learning tools and that they specifically facilitate comprehension and retention in multiple, complex ways. We will explore
this literature in the context of how the graphic syllabus and the outcomes
map can enhance students' understanding of the course and the subject matter
and, to an extent, their ability to learn.

The Pedagogical Power of Graphics: The Evidence

The research on the effects of graphics on student learning focuses on two different kinds of graphics: concept maps, also called graphic organizers, and
mind maps. Both types spatially display the relationships among ideas and
concepts, and both have proven to be potent pedagogical tools, but they differ
in several ways.

Concept Maps

Concept maps are a general class of graphics that can take on multiple shapes.
They follow no particular framework or template for organizing knowledge.
Angelo and Cross (1993) describe them as "drawings or diagrams showing the
mental connections that students make between a major concept . . . and other
concepts they have learned" (p. 197) when they proposed using concept maps
as a classroom assessment technique.

Concept maps are often structured like a network or spider web in which any concept or idea can be connected to any other. They may be organized around one or more central ideas to illustrate general associations, comparisons, contrasts, categorical relationships, hierarchical relationships, causal relationships, or logical relationships. Where a relationship is not obvious in the spatial context, the connecting line should be labeled to specify the relationship.

A concept map can show a process or sequencing of events, in which case the map takes the form of a chain or flowchart. Concept maps can even represent a continuum or a pyramid. In fact, concept maps don't follow any rules as to their shape or the connections they may depict. Graphic syllabi and outcomes maps fall under the broad category of concept maps. A graphic syllabus in particular can incorporate metaphors, icons, and other unique artistic features that concept maps normally don't have.

In numerous studies, concept maps have proven very helpful in developing students' cognitive skills, such as postsecondary reading comprehension (Katayama, 1997; Mealy & Nist, 1989; Robinson & Kiewra, 1995; Robinson & Schraw, 1994), critical thinking (King & Shell, 2002; Nixon-Cobb, 2005; Schuster, 2000; West, Pomeroy, Park, Gerstenberger, & Sandoval, 2000; Wilkes, Cooper, Lewin, & Batts, 1999), and problem solving (Baugh & Mellot, 1998; Beissner, 1992).

Concept maps have helped college students master many disciplines, including accounting (Leauby & Brazina, 1998), applied statistics (Schau & Mattern, 1997), biology (Briscoe & LaMaster, 1991; Cliburn, 1990; Kinchin, 2000, 2001; Wallace & Mintzes, 1990), chemistry (Regis & Albertazzi, 1996), conceptual astronomy (Zeilik et al., 1997), geoscience (Rebich & Gautier, 2005), mathematics (Brinkmann, 2003), nursing (Baugh & Mellott, 1998; King & Shell, 2002; Schuster, 2000; Wilkes et al., 1999), and medicine (Hoffman, Trott, & Neely, 2002; McGaghie, McCrimmon, Mitchell, Thompson, & Ravitch, 2000; West et al., 2000), among others.

Zeilik et al. (1997) found that astronomy students who used concept maps scored higher than the control group on three types of concept-based tests: a set of multiple-choice items designed to pinpoint misconceptions, a fill-in concept map, and a test of the ability to relate concepts.

Some researchers speculate that concept maps are so effective, at least in part, because of the constructivist and interactive way that many instructors use them. For example, some instructors not only provide concept maps to help students understand material, but they also have students develop concept maps along with the instructor, in peer groups, or on their own. In this latter context, students are actively constructing their own knowledge

(Kinchin, 2000, 2001), organizing it (Hoffman et al., 2002; McGaghie et al., 2000), and integrating it with prior knowledge (Plotnick, 2001).

The graphics that students produce help them clarify their thinking, reinforce their understanding of the material, and identify any misconceptions they may have (Vojtek & Vojtek, 2000). These graphics give instructors insight into their students' misconceptions and their cognitive progress in structuring knowledge in complex and appropriate ways (Romance & Vitale, 1997).

Mind Maps

In contrast to concept maps, mind maps conform to distinct rules. They are always organized around one central concept or idea and always follow a tree structure that clearly distinguishes among the primary, secondary, and tertiary ideas. In addition, they use icons, color, line thickness, and similar effects to communicate meaning, whereas concept maps may use but don't depend on any of these features. Similarly, graphic syllabi and outcomes maps may borrow the visual cues of mind maps, but they don't have to.

The mind-mapping technique was developed by Buzan (1974, 1991) as a note-taking technique. It was then popularized by Ellis (2000), among others, as a tool to help students organize material for study, review, and writing assignments. The technique is simple: Write the main concept in the center of the page and draw lines with related ideas radiating from the center in any direction. All the words written on the map should be *key* words (nouns or verbs) that represent the most concise and focused way to capture the idea. Additional supporting concepts may radiate from the secondary concepts. You should make central lines thicker than the supporting ones, make each major branch a different color, and add suggestive icons and symbols wherever possible.

Instructors have found mind maps to be successful teaching aids in finance (Biktimirov & Nilson, 2006), business (Driver, 2001), economics (Nettleship, 1992), marketing (Eriksson & Hauer, 2004), business statistics (Sirias, 2002), executive education (Mento, Martinelli, & Jones, 1999), and optometry (McClain, 1987). In medicine, a study conducted on 50 second- and third-year medical students found that using mind mapping to study improved the students' factual recall of text one week after reading it (Farrand, Hussain, & Hennessy, 2002).

Several major literature reviews have amassed abundant evidence that visual displays in any number of forms enhance learning (e.g., Vekiri, 2002; Winn, 1991). Constructivist theory gives us a good idea of how graphics work when students themselves develop the graphics. But how do grahics help students learn when they are provided to the students? How do the graphic syllabus and the outcomes map communicate a course more effectively to students? The following section explains what we know about how graphics produce learning benefits.

Reaching Visual, Global, and Intuitive Learning Styles

Researchers have developed more than a dozen learning-style models based on different dimensions in which the human mind can vary: sensory modalities, information processing, multiple intelligences, personality/psychological types, cognitive styles, experiential preferences, and orientations to learning (Theall, 1997). The pedagogical point of all these models is that students learn material more easily and with greater retention when they receive it in one of the styles they prefer or depend on, or convert it themselves (Filbeck & Smith, 1996). It is likely that any given classroom contains a student population with the full range of learning styles. Therefore, we should use diverse communication, teaching, and assessment strategies that will give as many students as possible a good chance to learn and to demonstrate their mastery.

Almost all of these learning style models posit one or two types or styles that process visually presented material more readily than the same material presented in another medium. These types include visual, visual-kinesthetic, concrete, visual-spatial, global, holistic, artistic, intuitive-feeling, and diverger. Traditionally, postsecondary education has been pitched to the more verbal, digital, rational, logical, abstract, sequential, and analytic styles, as are standard textbooks, typical digital presentations, lectures, and text syllabi. Unless a student is both visual and verbal in orientation, he or she will find it difficult to attend to, process, and retain materials that are presented in text form alone.

By showing how concepts and processes interrelate in terms of spatial relationships, images, colors, and codes, graphics help instructors reach their visual, global, and concrete learners, who tend to think in pictorial, spatial, and sensate terms (Clark & Paivio, 1991; Fleming & Mills, 1992; Svinicki, 2004; Theall, 1997). These are the students least likely to gain and retain information from a standard text syllabus. Visual aids help them process knowledge at a deep rather than a surface level (Svinicki, 2004). Imagine how these students can profit by understanding the organization of their course material at a deep level.

The following sections draw on the dual coding theory, the visual argument theory, and cognitive theory to explain why graphics are so effective. But these three theories claim that *all* people, not just those with certain learning styles, process and retain knowledge better when they receive it in a visual mode. Whatever a person's learning style, a well-constructed graphic is almost impossible to forget.

Dual-Coding Material into Memory

Before researchers starting mapping the brain, dual coding theory posited that the human mind has two memories, the semantic and the episodic, that correspond to the verbal and visual-spatial systems, respectively (Paivio, 1971). More recently, neuroscience and cognitive psychological research have found that people process and store verbal and visual-spatial information in separate cognitive systems (Vekiri, 2002), lending dual coding theory greater credibility. According to this theory and the research that supports it, graphics facilitate learning by enabling students to store knowledge in both systems, not just in the typical linguistic form, without overloading the working memory (Moreno & Mayer, 1999). Indeed, material received in both verbal and visual modalities tends to be retained better and longer than that received in only one form, and it can be accessed and retrieved more easily by two paths than it can by one (Kosslyn, 1994; Mayer & Gallini, 1990; Mayer & Sims, 1994; Paivio, 1971, 1990; Paivio & Csapo, 1973; Paivio, Walsh, & Bons, 1994; Svinicki, 2004; Tigner, 1999; Vekiri, 2002). A standard text syllabus engages only the semantic memory, but presenting a graphic syllabus and an outcomes map ensures that the students will encode the organization of the course onto their episodic memories as well.

Increasing the Efficiency of Learning and Retention

The visual argument theory previously mentioned hypothesizes that graphics such as concept and mind maps make material more memorable, but for a different reason—because graphics convey information more efficiently than text. They are more efficient in that they require less working memory and fewer cognitive transformations than text (Larkin & Simon, 1987; Robinson, Katayama, DuBois, & Devaney, 1998; Robinson & Kiewra, 1995; Robinson & Molina, 2002; Robinson & Schraw, 1994; Robinson & Skinner, 1996; Waller, 1981; Winn, 1987). Graphics are less taxing on the mind to comprehend, and people can also draw inferences from them more easily (Larkin & Simon, 1987).

Graphics work so economically because of what Larkin and Simon (1987) call "perceptual enhancement," which means they communicate information on two levels at once: through their individual elements and through the spatial arrangement of those elements. At the same time, all the relevant concepts and relationships, all the important information, are displayed simultaneously as a whole, giving the viewer a "computational advantage" (Larkin & Simon, 1987). The various elements are easy to locate, facilitating the extraction of information, and the interrelationships among the elements are evident in the spatial arrangements, shapes of enclosures, and colors, without the mind having to interpret or infer them.

Contrast the effortless, holistic process of visual perception with the slower and more complicated task of obtaining information by reading printed material. Text organizes and presents information hierarchically, one piece at a time, and the mind processes it sequentially, one piece at a time. Then the mind must work on and think about these pieces. They often require interpretation, and for any hope of retention, the mind has to distinguish the key pieces from the rest, then reorganize and assemble them into some kind of mental structure. This process requires a great deal of working memory and a series of cognitive transformations. Not only is it difficult—it inhibits the mind from doing anything else with the information, such as considering its implications, relating it to other material, evaluating its utility, or applying it to solve a problem. Even finding specific information in text is inefficient compared to locating it on a graphic, as the reader must search through paragraphs and even pages and perhaps refer to the table of contents or the index (Larkin & Simon, 1987; Veriki, 2002).

Dale Roy (cited in Gedalof, 1998) of McMaster University orchestrates a dramatic demonstration of how much more memorable graphics are than text. During his seminar on lecturing, he has participants develop two transparencies—one text-based and the other an image—and give a brief oral presentation on each one. The results are consistent. The academic audience, a group highly skilled in processing text, can reconstruct just about all of the image-based presentation but can recall no more than half of the text-based one.

By extrapolation, then, a text syllabus alone is not a very efficient way to communicate information about a course.

Another benefit of graphics, one that is particularly important in the global village we now inhabit, is that they communicate across cultures. Many of the conventions used in visuals, such as spatial proximity among closely related elements and the use of arrows to indicate direction or movement, seem to be universal. So it appears that at least some of these conventions are anchored in the basic human processes of visual perception (Tversky, 1995, 2001).

Showing the Structural Big Picture

A well-crafted graphic can supply a ready-made global organization for the mind to assimilate and store new knowledge. Learners with the global or the holistic learning style need to see this overarching organization of the whole before they can learn the pieces. In other words, they must see the structure of the new knowledge before they can process the components of it. For them, big-picture graphics level the playing field. These learners may indeed be more dependent than others on having an organization framework up front, but according to cognitive theory, *all* learners need this kind of cognitive scaffolding. The human mind will not store new material unless it is structured in some logical way.

However, some minds are better than others at logically organizing new information and knowledge. As we considered in Chapter 1, we are experts with a sound content background and a well-grounded structure of prior knowledge for assimilating new knowledge. In fact, expert thinking is distinguished by working from a conceptual organization of knowledge (Anderson, 1993; Carey, 1985; Chi, Glaser, & Rees, 1982; Novak, 1977). This organization anchors the expert's understanding of the interrelationships among concepts, facts, data, and principles as stated (or drawn) in the form of propositions (e.g., heat causes molecules to move faster) (Alexander, 1996).

On the other hand, our students come to us as novices with little prior knowledge and disciplinary language, and sometimes with faulty models and assorted misconceptions about the subject matter (Svinicki, 2004). Novice learners have no basis for correctly discerning the central, core concepts and principles of a discipline (Kozma, Russell, Jones, Marx, & Davis, 1996). As a result, they roam around a body of knowledge in an unsystematic, uncomprehending way, learning material superficially and often incorrectly, memorizing isolated facts and vocabulary, and trying to solve problems and answer questions by trial and error (Glaser, 1991). They fail to recognize the patterns, generalizations, abstractions, and algorithms that are second nature to the expert, and without these, they cannot apply what knowledge they do have to solving problems at a conceptual level (de Jong & Ferguson-Hessler, 1996).

To move beyond novice status and develop the deep understanding of the expert, a learner must acquire a valid hierarchical schema for organizing disciplinary knowledge. From the previous discussion, it follows that this schema must meet certain criteria. First, it must be convincing enough to override the learner's previous misconceptions, if any, about the subject matter. Second, it must accurately represent the basic paradigm of the discipline, or it will not accommodate new knowledge. Third, it must be comprehensive enough to encompass multiple conceptual networks. Finally, it must be hierarchical in order to distinguish the more general and core concepts and propositions from the derivative and condition-specific. In the view of many cognitive science researchers, deep, meaningful learning is nothing more and nothing less than progress in developing a robust conceptual understanding of the structure of knowledge (Reif & Heller, 1982; Royer, Cisero, & Carlo, 1993).

The odds of a learner developing such a schema on his or her own are poor. It is incumbent on experts—that is, college instructors—to guide the learner through an intellectual apprenticeship (Kozma et al., 1996). We might reflect on how and when we acquired our well-grounded disciplinary structure. It probably took years of study, culminating in graduate school, where we read and discussed our field extensively and apprenticed with one or more faculty members. Whether or not we learned with the help of conceptual maps, we eventually assembled a schema for organizing and storing our specialized knowledge. Unlike us, most of our students will not study our discipline long enough to develop a sound structure. Many will just be passing through it for a semester or two. Without structure, they will process our course content superficially and quickly forget it. Shouldn't we then make our organization of the knowledge we teach *explicit* by providing students with an accurate, ready-made structure for making sense of the knowledge and storing it?

The most effective and concise way to convey that big-picture organization is with an "advance organizer," which may be any type of graphic, and should precede the introduction of more detailed content (Ausubel, 1968; Carlile & Jordan, 2005). Some educators (Anderson, 1984; Leichhardt, 1989; Romance & Vitale, 1999) specifically recommend concept maps for this purpose because they most clearly and flexibly display the structure of knowledge and the integration of its elements. Their suggestion makes sense, as the last two criteria for a sound working schema—its ability to integrate multiple conceptual networks and its hierarchical structure—are characteristic of web-shaped concept maps, as well as mind maps.

Regardless of what visual is used, it should clearly lay out the relationships among key concepts and dimensions and highlight the most central and important ones. A good graphical representation will help students 1) focus on the conceptual relationships, rather than on the memorization of terms; 2) recognize patterns among concepts; 3) infer new, complex relationships, thereby elaborating on the schema; and 4) integrate the new information into the knowledge structure they already have. And a graphic will enhance learning in all these ways more effectively than text (Hyerle, 1996; Robinson et al., 1998; Robinson & Kiewra, 1995; Robinson & Schraw, 1994; Robinson & Skinner, 1996; Winn, 1991).

Without a sense of the structure of the content, what sense can students make of the course schedule in the syllabus? If they cannot discern the relationships among the topics, the week-by-week development and elaboration of the subject matter just looks like a list of disconnected terms. It is at this time in the course, the very beginning, that students can most benefit from something like an advance organizer.

Perhaps those of you who review the syllabi of faculty from other disciplines are familiar with this confusion and disorientation that an "alien" text syllabus can produce. Reading the schedule of course topics and the student learning objectives is like trying to decipher written directions on how to get from one unidentified, unconnected place to another, with no destination clearly in mind. Or it is like trying to guess from a grocery list exactly what major meal someone plans to prepare. How can students acquire and retain knowledge and abilities without having a valid, overarching structure in which to place them? It seems well worth the effort to present the organization of a course so that students can understand, appreciate, and follow it.

Extending the two analogies above, a graphic syllabus is like a well-labeled map that supplements the written driving directions, and an outcomes map is like a flowchart that shows how ingredients combine to compose a complete meal. Without word-laden explanations, both tools reveal exactly how and implicitly *why* a course is organized in a particular way. The graphic syllabus charts the "flow" between topics and concepts and makes the big picture of the course structure evident. It shows how the trees are arranged to create the forest. The outcomes map charts the "flow" of learning from the more basic skills and abilities students are expected to acquire to the more advanced ones. It shows the cumulative structure of the learning process—how skills and abilities build on each other and combine to enable students to accomplish more complex and professional-level tasks.

Of course, the point of presenting the course organization graphically is not to help students remember the course design per se, but to help them retain the overall organization of the course material. Because structure is the glue that makes knowledge adhere in the mind, students' memory of the course organization should help them retain the course content as well. Otherwise, the material will quickly fade away from memory like so many irrelevant factoids.

Helping Students Accomplish Tasks

Concept mapping and mind mapping have proven useful in many cognitive activities that involve memorizing, planning, organizing, and creating, such as outlining papers and oral presentations, project managing, problem solving, managing meetings, organizing and summarizing material for tests, and even creative writing (Buzan, 1974; Svinicki, 2004; Wycoff, 1991). These techniques foster creativity by engaging both the verbal-analytical and visual-holistic sides of the brain, thereby freeing the mind from the constraints of linear thinking and releasing the flow of new ideas. If we want to teach our students not only our subject matter but also efficient methods for learning it and creative ways of using it, we can provide students with helpful models, such as a graphic syllabus and an outcomes map, for visually organizing material. We can then teach them the underlying principles of mind maps and concept maps and their many proven, practical applications.

The Pedagogical Potential of Graphics

Graphics have a way of freeing us from conventions. I have conducted a two- to three-hour workshop on designing a graphic syllabus more than 15 times for faculty groups in several universities and at a variety of conferences in three different countries, and I have seen instructors add humor and expressions of their personality to a graphic syllabus that they wouldn't think of inserting into a text syllabus. In Chapter 3 and Appendix A, you will find many examples of such novelty in the form of clip art and original icons, drawings, and pictures.

Whimsical touches in instructional materials are more than just cute and fun. From what we know about how the mind works, they aid learning by attracting attention and reinforcing new synaptic connections. Novelty and anything that evokes emotion attracts attention (Mangurian, 2005). In addition, emotional arousal releases chemicals from the limbic system into the brain that reinforce associated synaptic connections. This means that when students feel emotions as they are cognitively processing new material, they learn that material more readily and retain it longer (Leamnson, 2000; Mangurian, 2005). In other words, if we can evoke emotions in our students, we can facilitate their learning.

We needn't arouse strong emotions. In fact, the mind often represses experiences associated with high stress, great discomfort, deep conflict, and trauma, and thereby inhibits retrieval. The emotions that foster learning are positive, motivating, and not at all paralyzing: wonder, fascination, intrigue, curiosity, surprise, challenge, compassion, and humor. Well-crafted, engaging learning experiences—the case method, problem-based learning, role-playing, simulations and games, service-learning, field work, clinicals—typically evoke such feelings, as do collaborative experiences and reflective writing assignments. But so do the "small" experiences, such as the amusement at seeing a smiley face or funny-looking stick figure on a handout.

Adding personal touches to instructional materials, such as a graphic syllabus, says good things about you: that you have a sense of humor, that you're open to novel ideas, that you're at ease with students and your role as instructor, and that you care enough about your students to make an extra effort to reach them. Students *want* an instructor with these qualities. They can relate to such an individual, whatever the age difference. Furnishing your students with visual learning aids such as a graphic syllabus and an outcomes map shows that you care about them and respect them enough to have carefully constructed your course for them. In addition, you are helping them understand and appreciate how and why you've constructed your course the way you have. What an excellent way to begin your relationship with your class!

3

Designing a Graphic Syllabus

A graphic syllabus can be defined as a flowchart or diagram that displays the sequencing and organization of major course topics through the semester. Much like a concept map or mind map, it uses spatial arrangement, connecting lines, arrows, and sometimes numbers to show the logical, temporal progression of the course through topics within the subject matter. In addition, it may—but need not—use icons, pictures, and visual metaphors to convey the meaning of words, concepts, and relationships.

Being verbal and rational, definitions serve their purpose well for understanding verbal, left-brain entities such as concepts and principles, but they are less effective at describing visual, right-brain phenomena. For instance, we can define a *drawing,* a *painting,* or a *sculpture* in so many words, but we don't really understand what any of these things are unless we see examples of them and experience the thoughts and feelings they evoke. So rather than work from the definition of a graphic syllabus, we might learn more by working inductively and studying a few examples. This way we can acquire an experience-based, intuitive understanding of what a graphic syllabus is and how it lays out the big picture.

Figure 3.1 is a graphic "syllabus" of this book. Granted that this book is not a course; it is something with which you, the reader, are familiar. It has an organization, a logical flow, that might not be evident from the table of contents, the chapter headings, and the subheadings. What "hides" the internal organization is inherent in the nature of a book—its message is presented linearly, piece by piece, as though it is a one-dimensional string of ideas. In the case of a novel, the structure is already a given; it's in the story, which the human mind is primed to remember. But an expository work has no given structure, and the organization is whatever "logic" the author improvises to best communicate his or her message. Unless the author makes the organization explicit, it may take a savvy reader to decipher the structure.

Figure 3.1

Graphic "Syllabus" of This Book

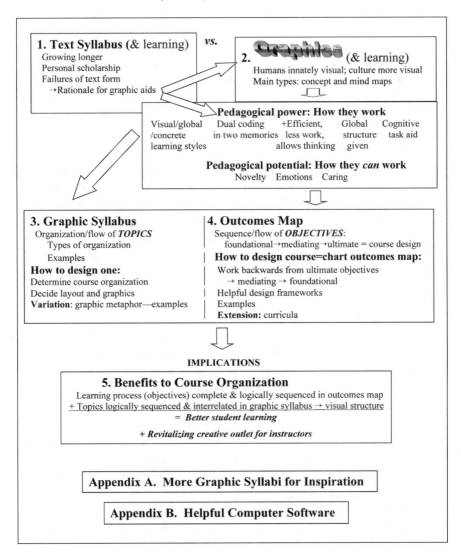

A graphic can make a book's organization explicit in a way that a table of contents can't. As the graphic of this book shows, Chapters 1 and 2 not only address the topics in the subheadings but also draw an implicit contrast between text and graphics as learning media. Together they justify turning to graphics to "say" what technical words alone cannot convey to the novice.

This justification made, the reader should now be interested in finding out more about the specific graphic tools proposed in this book to communicate a course.

The graphic syllabus and outcomes map are addressed in parallel—first with definitions and illustrative examples, then with strategies to design them, including the choices among options that must be made in the design process. At this point, the reader understands how graphics facilitate learning and, at least theoretically, how to design a graphic syllabus and an outcomes map to reflect the structure of a course. He or she can now appreciate the implications of these tools for improving course design and development: ensuring that the student learning process is complete and appropriately sequenced, and providing students with a cohesive, logically organized structure for assimilating and retaining the course material. Instructors also gain personally through the opportunity to express their scholarship in a creative new venue. The book then provides additional annotated examples of graphic syllabi and concludes with information on available software for designing a graphic syllabus and an outcomes map.

Types of Expository Structures

The logic of this book's structure is only one of many possible logics for organizing a long piece of expository writing. Courses, too, are expository works of scholarship that may follow any one of many possible logics for organizing a body of knowledge for learning purposes. They can be structured as a debate between competing schools of thought, and this debate may reveal complementarities between them. They can arrange topics around the parallel relationships between different phenomena. They can be organized as a process by which something happens or by which we accomplish a task. They can follow a sequence or chronology. Or they can present knowledge in a hierarchy of increasingly refined categories. No doubt other kinds of logics are available and used.

Unfortunately for teaching and learning, courses have the same weaknesses as books in that their organization is usually hidden, at least to the novice, by the linear, piece-by-piece way that students encounter the topics throughout the semester. Furthermore, the list-bound schedule of topics displayed by the text syllabus only reinforces the illusion that the discipline is merely a one-dimensional string of subjects, rather than an organic, interwoven body of abstract concepts, principles, and relationships.

Graphics, however, provide an easy way to clarify the logical flow of a course by displaying the subject matter as a debate, as parallel tracks, as a process, as a sequence or chronology, or as a hierarchy of categories. Let's examine some graphic syllabi that exemplify each kind of course structure.

Competition and Complementarity

Most of us can identify areas of study that are the battlegrounds for competing theories. In English and comparative literature, at least three schools of thought—the rational, the symbolic interpretive, and the postmodern—contend for prominence. In philosophy, determinism, free willism, compatibilism, and fatalism represent conflicting world views of what makes people and their lives what they are. Foreign language education has entertained debates among numerous approaches: the Silent Method, Rassias' Dartmouth Method, the Natural Method, and the Total Physical Response Method. Many perspectives in K–12 education have emerged over the years, including the self-esteem approach, the constructivist method, the traditional method, the New Math, Natural Math, Fuzzy Math, and the discovery method. Some have even been reported in the national media. In political science, pluralism and elitism compete for credibility. In sociology, their counterparts are functionalism and conflict theory. In social science epistemology, the contenders are positivism and phenomenology. In medicine and health science, they are the mechanistic and the holistic. While usually dominated by one paradigm, areas of the biological, geological, and physical sciences also become battlegrounds for opposing theories at times.

Competing theories can provide an organizational strategy for an entire course. This type of structure can encompass many topics: 1) the different issues addressed by each theory, thereby encompassing the full range of issues addressed by the discipline; 2) the empirical or analytic works each has generated, thus providing room for the defining works of the disciplines; 3) the methodologies each school typically uses, thereby revealing the strengths, weaknesses, and biases of various research and analytical methods; and 4) the paradoxical research findings from which each side draws its evidence, which bring to light the complexity of the phenomena under study, the uncertainties within the discipline, and the limits that any one perspective imposes on the quest for truth.

The first graphic syllabus that I know of, which is the first one I ever designed, was organized around competing theories. It was for the course Sociology 123: Social Stratification, which I taught regularly for several years at the University of California–Los Angeles. No decent textbook on the topic was available, so I developed the course from scratch, including its unique organization. I structured it to show how functionalism and conflict theory don't contradict each other as much as they address different issues (types of inequality) using different methodological strategies. It's not surprising that the theories have seemingly contradictory findings that depict very different social orders—one based in value consensus and the other in elite-class domination.

The course topics are listed in Figure 3.2 just as they appeared in the text syllabus, only without the reading assignments. If you cannot discern the course structure from the list, you are not alone; neither could my students. The structure was invisible to everyone but me. After teaching the course a few times, I channeled my frustration into drawing a flowchart of the substantive organization of the course, shown in Figure 3.3, and distributed the flowchart to the class along with the text syllabus. I noticed that the students actually studied the document and referred to it during the term. I also referred to it as we progressed through the topics.

Figure 3.2

Weekly Topics in SOC 123:
Social Stratification,
Dr. Linda B. Nilson, Circa 1980

Week-by-Week List of Topics, Quarter System

Weeks 1 & 2: What Social Stratification Is—Across Species, Through History, and According to Consensus Theory (Functionalism), Conflict Theory, and Lenski's Attempt at Synthesis

Week 3:   Inequalities in Wealth and Income

Week 4:   Inequalities in Power

Week 5:   Review and Midterm

Week 6:   Inequalities in Prestige; Measurements of Socioeconomic Status

Week 7:   Inequality of Opportunity for Wealth, Income, Power, and Prestige: Social Mobility and Status Attainment

Weeks 8 & 9: How Modern Stratification Persists: The Political System—Wealthfare, Welfare, and Pluralistic Representative Democracy

Week 10:   How Modern Stratification Persists: People's Beliefs and Subjective Responses to Stratification

Week 11:   Final Examination

Figure 3.3
Graphic Syllabus of SOC 123: Social Stratification,
Dr. Linda B. Nilson, Circa 1980.
Type of Organization: Competition and Complementarity

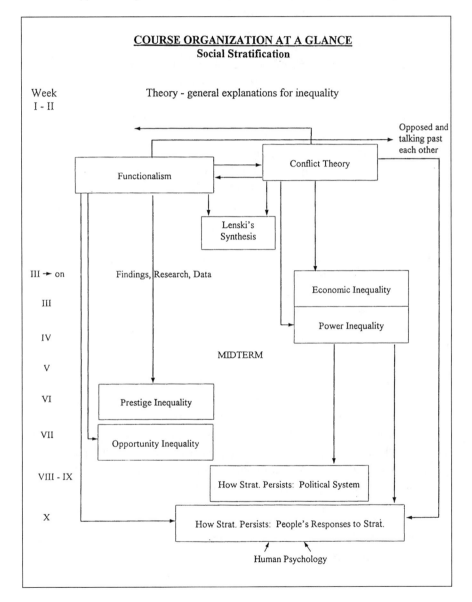

Although students didn't suddenly perform better on tests, a few of them commented that they used the graphic syllabus and better understood the course because of it, so I continued using it. In the early 1980s, instructors didn't conduct classroom research to assess the impact of new teaching tools, nor did they discuss teaching with their colleagues, especially at research universities. As a result, my idea went underground for about 15 years.

The graphic syllabus of my Social Stratification course shows that functionalism spawns research on inequalities in prestige and opportunity, which are measured in representative national surveys on a continuous quantitative (ordinal) scale. On the other hand, conflict theorists study economic and political inequalities, which the historical, documentary, and quantitative economic data that they use indicate are highly concentrated in a small elite class in most types of societies. Along with psychology, functionalism and conflict theory both contribute explanations for why social stratification persists, although conflict theory offers more and richer reasons. All in all, the two schools of thought complement each other, each filling in the knowledge the other fails to generate. The branch that shows Lenski's attempt to synthesize the two theories seems to die out, which is exactly what happened to Lenski's attempt in real life.

Of course, some instructors in disciplines with competing theories decide not to explicate the debate but rather to address only one side, typically the side to which they belong. They structure their courses somewhat like a rhetorical essay—claim, evidence, warrant—in favor of their own perspective. Certainly they have the right to do so. But they do so at a cost to the students. In contrast to the course organized around competing schools of thought, the one-sided course examines only some of the discipline's issues and only some of the defining works. A student learns only some of the discipline's methodologies and probably not their weaknesses and biases. Moreover, the learner acquires a simplistic perspective of the phenomena under study, one that might pass for "right" and "certain" to the novice, feeding the dualistic thinking (Perry, 1968) from which we try to free students. Any one perspective spotlights just one facet of a phenomenon and disguises the fact that reality is more complex and messy than any human interpretation of it.

Parallelism

Some areas of study lend themselves to parallel presentation. For instance, Dr. Cynthia Desrochers, professor of education and founding director of the Center for Excellence in Teaching and Learning at California State University–Northridge, organized her elementary education course, Methods of Teaching Language Arts and History-Social Science, to highlight the "match" between the school curriculum—that is, the skills and abilities the schools aim to develop in students—and the strategies used for instruction and assessment. As a result, Dr. Desrochers's future teachers studied the content of the curriculum in language arts and history-social science at the same time they were learning ways to teach the content and to assess their future students' mastery of it.

Figure 3.4 shows Dr. Desrochers's graphic syllabus for her course. The parallel arrangement is more than a matter of convenience; it carries the message that student learning objectives, teaching methods, and assessment instruments must be consonant with each other. However, this message does not come through in the text syllabus shown in Figure 3.5.

Figure 3.4

Graphic Syllabus of EED 570M: Methods of Teaching
Language Arts and History-Social Science,
Dr. Cynthia Desrochers, 2000.
Type of Organization: Parallelism

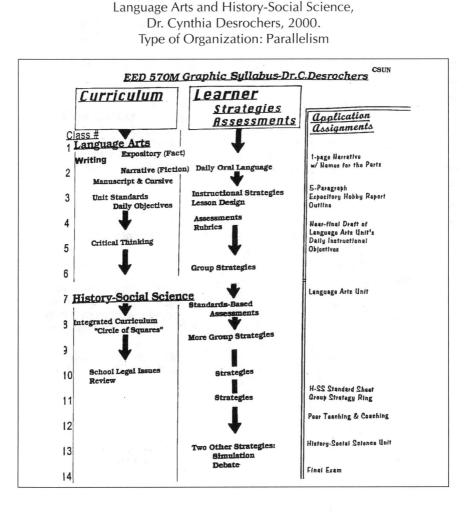

Figure 3.5 (page 1)

Text Syllabus of EED 570M:
Methods of Teaching Language Arts and History-Social Science,
Dr. Cynthia Desrochers, 2000

Course Schedule

** All assigned readings should be done prior to class sessions.

Session Topics	Readings/Assignments
Class #1-- 1/29	
Teaching Decisions	1. 5-Paragraph Report/Hobby
Language Arts	with self-photo. Bring
. The Writing Process	copies for all classmates.
. Expository Writing - Fact	Due: 2/5, N= 26 copies
	2. Bring a short narrative to
	next class, 1/31, write
	analysis of the "parts."
	N=6 copies
	3. Notebook- Make Table of
	Contents. Bring notebook
	to class daily.
Class #2 -- 1/31	
Narrative - Fiction	1. Have previewed Tompkins
Daily Oral Lang. (DOL)	2. Have read Desroch 34-101,
L.A. Unit Assigned	26-33, 1-7, 152-169,
Standard & In'al Objs.	and made a detailed Table
Due: 1/12	of Contents for entire
	notebook - due: 2/7.
Unit due: 2/19 (2 copies)	
Class #3 -- 2/5	
Unit Standards	1. Have read 38.10(& see www)
Daily Instructional Objectives	2. Report copies w/3 holes!
Elements of Lesson Design	
Assemble Hobby Reports	
Class #4 -- 2/7	
Student Assessment	1. Bring creative Report cover.
Rubrics	2. Analyze model rubrics in
	course notebook carefully!
	3. T. of C. for notebook due
Class #5 -- 2/12	
Critical Thinking	1. Have read Desroch 8-17
L.A. Unit Refinement	2. Have read Desroch 18-25
Bring "final" draft of	
Standard & In'al Objs.	
to class.	
Class #6 -- 2/14	
Group Strategies	1. Have skimmed Kagan
Group Strategy Ring Assigned	BRING Kagan to class
due: 3/5	2. Check Kagan Web site:
	<http://www.KaganOnline.com

Figure 3.5 (page 2)

Class #7 -- 2/19

    History--Social Science

    . "Standards-Based"

    . Assessments

        1. <u>Have read Desroch 102-151</u>

        2. <u>Have read Desroch 170-192</u>

        3. **<u>L.A. Unit Due Today(N=2)</u>**

           Prepare to share yours

Class #8 -- 2/21

    Integrated Curriculum

    "Circle of Squares"

    History--Soc.Sci. Unit Assigned

    Unit due: 3/12

    Submit 2 copies in large,

    self-addressed envelope and

    sufficient postage to return

    one unit to you via US mail.

Class #9 -- 2/26

    More Group Strategies

    Strategies as SDAIE

    Peer Teaching/Coaching Assigned

    due: 3/7

Class #10 -- 2/28

    Review for Final

    Legal Issues

        1. <u>Have **STUDIED** class notes</u>

        2. <u>Have read Desroch 239-257</u>

Class #11 -- 3/5

    History--S.S. Unit Refinement **Strategy Ring due**

    Bring "final" draft of your

    Analysis of a Standard Sheet

Class #12 -- 3/7

    Peer Teaching & Coaching

    today...FUN!

    AKA, "Putting it <u>all</u> together!"

Class #13 -- 3/12

    Two Other Strategies: **History--S.S. Unit due**

    Simulations   (2 copies in large envelope

    Debate   with sufficient postage)

Class #14 -- 3/14

    Final Exam today   Bring a good pen, white-out,

                      and grade postcard. I will

                      provide the paper.

Another interesting feature of Dr. Desrochers's graphic syllabus that is not obvious is the spacing between the application assignments. The amount of white space beneath each one provided students with a rough gauge of the amount of time they have to complete it (C. Desrochers, personal correspondence, November 16, 2006).

The following semester, Dr. Desrochers developed another graphic syllabus for her course based on the creation of one of her students. For this version, see Figure A.4 in Appendix A.

Dr. Jan Williams Murdoch, professor of psychology and dean of undergraduate studies at Clemson University, structured her Clinical Practicum to spotlight the parallels between professional relationships and relationships with clients in clinical psychology. As shown in Dr. Murdoch's graphic syllabus in Figure 3.6, the two sets of relationships impact each other at crucial junctures. Supervision and peer supervision shape the legal and ethical side of client relationships, while clinical record keeping affects risk management (and indirectly, clinician stress and self-care) on the professional side.

Process

Some courses are developed around a process, which is a series of occurrences, operations, or actions that ends in a particular result. Courses can be *about* a process, usually historical or developmental, such as the process by which societies develop and modernize, the process by which science has advanced from Aristotle to today, the process by which children's cognitive abilities develop, or the process by which species diversify. Or courses can aim to *teach* a process—that is, their main learning outcome is that students are able to perform a process—for example, how to diagnose and treat diseases; how to diagnose and troubleshoot problems in organizations, systems, or equipment; how to use engineering principles in forensic contexts; how to solve certain kinds of mathematical problems; how to design a physical structure, a communication system, or an information system; how to teach effectively; how to cook professionally; or how to conduct a research project. This last type of course is more common than the previous examples, no doubt.

Dr. Hugh D. Spitler's epidemiology course at Clemson University leads students through the process of doing epidemiology research, as his graphic syllabus in Figure 3.7 clearly shows. After the first exam, each large box represents a step in the research process, from defining suitable measurements, to finding appropriate theories to guide the analysis, to locating, then generating, and finally interpreting data. Students practice these steps on an outbreak investigation project.

Figure 3.6
Graphic Syllabus of PSYC 439: Clinical Practicum,
Dr. Jan Williams Murdoch, 2000.
Type of Organization: Parallelism

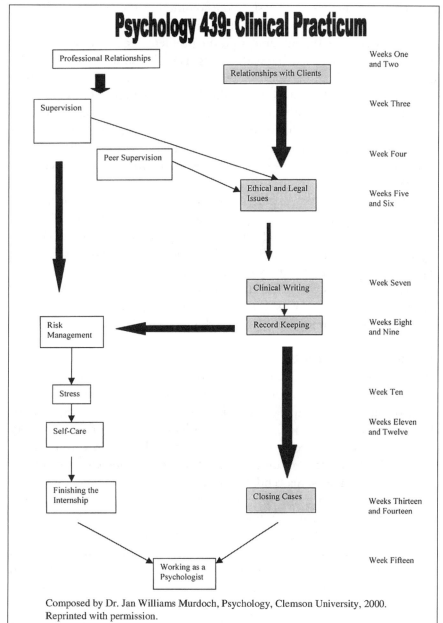

Composed by Dr. Jan Williams Murdoch, Psychology, Clemson University, 2000.
Reprinted with permission.

The process of planning a community health program is the subject of one of the courses that Dr. Vicki J. Ebin, associate professor of health education, teaches at California State University–Northridge. Her graphic syllabus shown in Figure 3.8 clearly maps out the succession of tasks in program planning: First, conducting an analysis of the community, then making a diagnosis, which defines a problem focus, followed by designing, administering, and analyzing needs assessment surveys on the problem. The final task involves planning the program, starting with setting its goals and objectives, then determining methods and activities, then deciding on the intervention strategies, and finally implementing and evaluating the program. The graphic also suggests that this series of tasks comprises the final project. Dr. Ebin's class schedule from her text syllabus (see Figure 3.9) lists the same topics in the same order as the graphic syllabus. However, the text schedule fails to clearly show the sequential connections between the topics that integrate them into a process.

Dr. Ebin also teaches Advanced Biostatistics for the Health Sciences as a process, as shown graphically in Figure 3.10. The process starts with developing a survey instrument that reflects community needs, moves on to collecting, entering, editing, and coding the data, and concludes with conducting one or more types of data analyses (univariate, bi-variate, multivariate)—a process that students will go through to complete a final project. Again, the text syllabus (see Figure 3.11) does not chunk the operations as the graphic does, nor does it communicate the research process as effectively.

Sequence/Chronology

A sequence or chronology is similar to a process in that both are a series of occurrences, operations, or actions. However, only a process culminates in an end product (e.g., a complete research project with results). A sequence or chronology is simply a succession of things based on logic or time. History courses, for an obvious example, are often structured around a chronology of events or developments over time. Certain historical phenomena, such as specific wars and dynasties, may end, but history doesn't.

Professor Dr. Aubrey Coffee in Clemson University's Department of Food Science organizes her Culinary Techniques course as a logical sequence of knowledge and skills that her students must master. Her graphic syllabus (see Figure 3.12) displays this quite clearly. After learning some history and the professional chef's role, students tackle the procedures and skills involved in safety and sanitation, including handling tools and equipment. These topics are so important that they must precede any other food-related activities. Then comes plate presentation and, finally, the principles of menu-building

Figure 3.7
Graphic Syllabus of HLTH 380: Epidemiology,
Dr. Hugh D. Spitler, 2001.
Type of Organization: Process

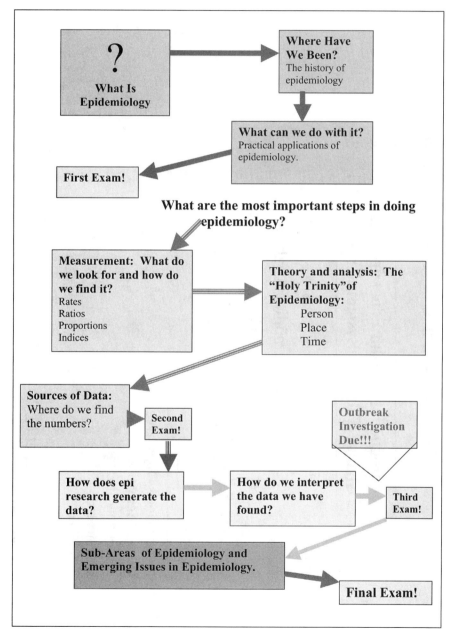

Figure 3.8

Graphic Syllabus of HSCI 441: Community Program Planning,
Dr. Vicki J. Ebin, 2005.
Type of Organization: Process

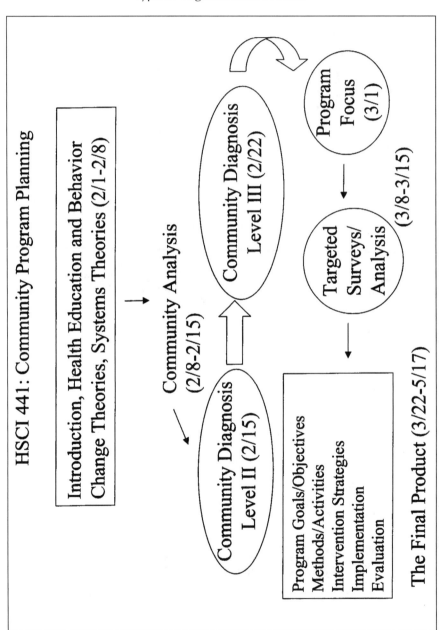

Figure 3.9

Text Syllabus of HSCI 441: Community Program Planning,
Dr. Vicki J. Ebin, 2005

Department of Health Science   California State University–Northridge
HSCI 441: Community Health Education   Spring Semester 2005

CLASS SCHEDULE

DATE	TOPIC	ASSIGNMENT
2/3	Introduction and course overview; Foundations of health education practice Community and Systems	
2/10	Planning models; Social Assessment and Participatory Planning *** Form Project Planning Teams**	Chapters 1, 2
2/17	Epidemiological Assessment; Health, Behavior, Environment	Chapter 3
2/24	Educational and Ecological Assessment	Chapter 4
3/3	Developing needs assessment surveys; Applications in Community Settings	Chapter 6
3/10	Needs assessment surveys (con't)/Survey analysis Program Goals and Objectives. Finalize Phase 1 of Team Project Paper	
3/17	**Midterm**	
3/24	Spring Break!	
3/31	Cesar Chavez Day Observance, no class	
4/7	Continue Goals & Objectives, Administrative & Policy Assessment Applications in Occupational Settings	Chapter 5 Chapter 7
4/14	Applications in Educational Settings- California Comprehensive School Health Education; Applications in Health Care Settings	Chapter 8 Chapter 9
4/21	Program Implementation, Social Marketing and Budgets	
4/28	Program Implementation (con't)	
5/5, 5/12	Program Evaluation	Chapter 5
5/19	Program Planning: Bringing it all together . . . *Course Review* *** Team Project Paper due at beginning of class**	
5/26	**Final Examination . . . Class meets at 5:30 p.m. SHARP!**	

Figure 3.10
Graphic Syllabus of HSCI 592:
Advanced Biostatistics for the Health Sciences,
Dr. Vicki J. Ebin, 2006.
Type of Organization: Process

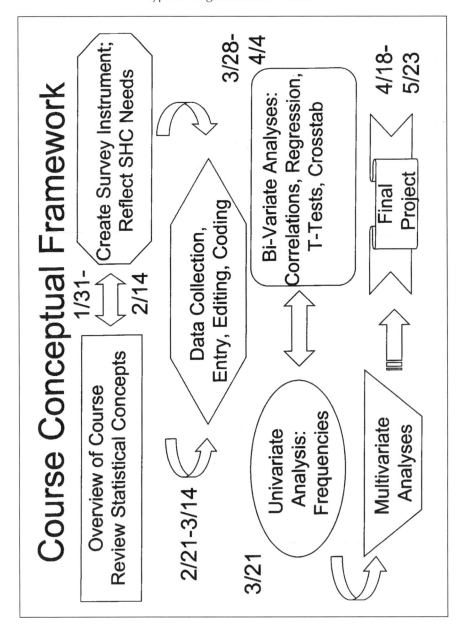

Figure 3.11

Text Syllabus of HSCI 592:
Advanced Biostatistics for the Health Sciences,
Dr. Vicki J. Ebin, 2006

Department of Health Science   California State University–Northridge
HSCI 592: Advanced Biostatistics for the Health Sciences   Spring Semester 2006
Dr. Vicki J. Ebin

Course Outline

Feb. 1	Overview of Course Content. Brainstorm possible topics and content areas for the research instrument. Prepare a literature review of possible content areas for the next class session. Begin computer tutorials. Overview of SPSS.
Feb. 8	Review Basic Concepts. Discuss research issues in study design and implementation. Small group discussion of content areas. Review basic statistical concepts. Read pp. 3–18, 421–440 (B), pp. 1–26 (D&M).
Feb. 15	Decisions of sampling. Group discussion of content areas. Finalize research instrument. More review of basic concepts. Read pp. 19–36 (B). **Assignment**: Write a research question based on the survey instrument, due Feb. 22nd.
Feb. 22	Begin data collection. Read pp. 37–58 (B), pp. 27–42 (D & M). **Assignment**: Describe the Conceptual Framework of your Research Proposal, due Mar. 1st.
Mar. 1	Continue data collection. Review data editing and coding. Discuss problems and issues. Read pp. 59–104 (B)
Mar. 8	Data entry. Read pp. 105–130 (B)
Mar. 15	Continue data entry. Data cleaning techniques. Read Guide Chapter 7. Read pp. 131–148 (B), pp. 43–66 (D&M). **Project Proposal due at the beginning of class**. **Assignment**: Frequencies of your research variables, due Mar. 22nd.
Mar. 22	Where do we start? Read pp. 149–168 (B), pp. 67–104 (D&M).
Mar. 29	Preliminary analyses. What questions are you asking. Read pp. 185–230 (B), 105–142, 221–132 (D&M). **Assignment**: t-tests, crosstabs (Chi Square), due Apr. 19th.
Apr. 5	Continue Crosstabs, bi-variate analyses. Read pp. 231–250 (B).
Apr. 12	Spring Break—no class!!!
Apr. 19	Linear Regression. Begin Multiple Regression. Read pp. 251–342 (B), pp. 177–206 (D & M). **Assignment**: Linear Regression, due Apr. 26th.
Apr. 26	Logistic Regression. Multiple Regression (con't). Read pp. 343–418 (B), 321–332 (D&M). **Assignment**: Logistic Regression, due May 3rd.
May 3	One-Way Analysis of Variance. Read pp. 143–152 (D&M). **Assignment**: One-Way ANOVA, due May 10th.
May 10	Two-Way Analysis of Variance. Read pp. 153–160 (D & M). **Assignment**: Two-Way ANOVA, due May 17th. Discussion of research findings and implications.
May 17, 24	Student Oral Presentations. **Papers due at the beginning of class.**

and cooking. The rest of the semester is devoted to the "course menu"—that is, the preparation of foods, sequenced from dairy products and eggs (with a breakfast focus), through the various courses of a dinner, to baked goods and desserts. By the end of the course, students are able to prepare an entire meal. This course organization may look like a process, but chefs do not prepare a meal in the order of the course menu. In fact, plating is the last thing they do before a meal is served, but this topic is addressed with other basic skills. Dr. Coffee enhances her graphic syllabus with appropriate icons.

Figure 3.13 shows the graphic syllabus I developed for the cross-disciplinary freshman seminar Free Will and Determinism, which I taught at Vanderbilt University in the 1990s. The list of topics out of the text syllabus was presented earlier in Chapter 1 to illustrate how alien the strictly text version of a course schedule can be to students. As both the graphic and the text list show, the first few weeks of the course focus on the philosophical definitions of, and arguments in favor and against, the different theories of what causes things to happen through life. Free will and determinism are only two of the theories. A philosophical hybrid of the two, compatibilism, is a third. Fatalism is yet another. (The umbrella-like figures above the key terms will be explained later.) Then the course leads students through classic readings that reflect each theory. The order of the reading topics follows a double sequence. From left to right, the readings move from deterministic to compatibilistic to free willist, and finally to fatalistic—specifically a contemporary version of fatalism called "spiritual destiny" in which fate is orchestrated by a higher power. But moving down from the sixth week of the semester, the sequence of readings reflects the history of philosophic trends over about 130 years, from the second half of the 19th century to the late 20th century.

Contrast the information communicated by the graphic syllabus with that conveyed by the text list of topics. Unless every reading were explicitly linked in the text list to the theory it reflects, the theory-based sequence of topics would not be as evident in the text syllabus as it is in the graphic. However, note that the historical sequence would probably be just as evident. When the order of topics follows a historical chronology, with the years or time periods clearly labeled, a careful reader should be able to discern the organization from the text syllabus alone.

Categorical Hierarchy

The last type of course structure we will examine is the organization of the material into a hierarchy of categories. This hierarchy could be one layer deep, in which case you might call the structure a "taxonomy," or it could be many layers deep, consisting of categories within categories. Let's begin with the

Figure 3.12
Graphic Syllabus of FDSC 215: Culinary Techniques,
Dr. Aubrey Coffee, 2006.
Type of Organization: Sequence/Chronology

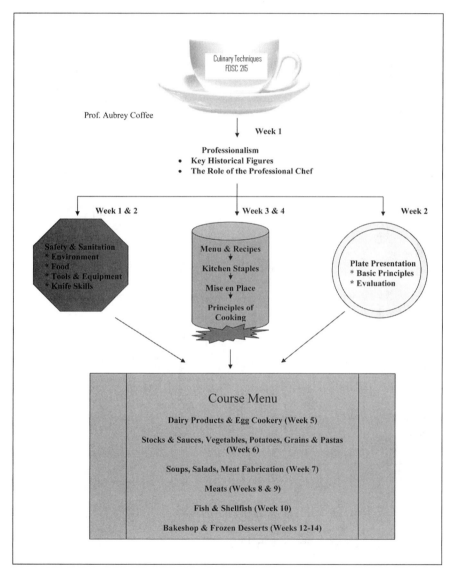

Figure 3.13

Graphic Syllabus of Freshman Seminar: Free Will and Determinism,
Dr. Linda B. Nilson, 1996.
Type of Organization: Sequence/Chronology

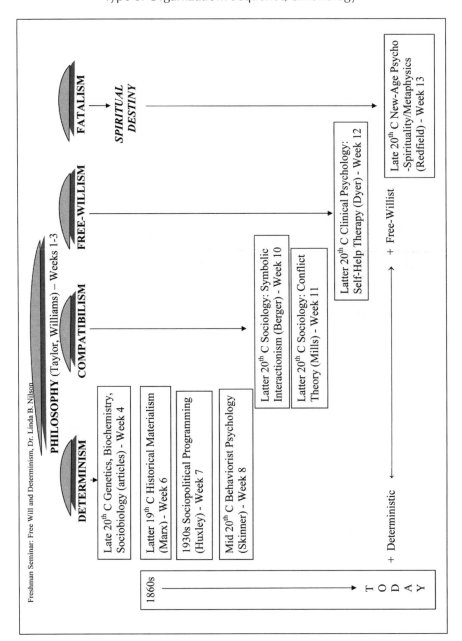

simplest one-layer type. Figure 3.14 shows the graphic syllabus that Dr. Robert W. Schwartz, professor of materials science and engineering at the University of Missouri–Rolla, developed for Ceramic and Materials Engineering (CME) 302: Phase Equilibria, while he taught at Clemson University. After the first week of introductory material on manufacturing and phase diagrams, the course is organized into three parts, one on each type of component system (primary, binary, and ternary). Dr. Schwartz arranges the boxes and the key information within them to resemble a matrix, which encourages students to draw comparisons and contrasts among the different systems. This graphic syllabus could probably double as a study sheet for the final exam.

A more complex example of a categorical hierarchy is Professor Laine Mears's graphic syllabus for ME 404: Manufacturing Processes and Their Application (see Figure 3.15). A member of the Department of Mechanical Engineering at Clemson, Dr. Mears first introduces students to the two categories of manufacturing, each of which has two subcategories. The rest of the course looks at three categories of manufacturing processes, each of which breaks down into more specific process categories, which in turn encompass even more specific operations. As categorical hierarchies go, this one is quite deep.

A final example of this type of structure is found in Figure 3.16, developed by Professor Carol Docan in the Department of Business Law at California State University–Northridge, for her course, BLAW 280: Business Law I. While this graphic syllabus generally reflects the course organization, it more precisely mirrors the way that Dr. Docan structures the field for teaching purposes. The numbers in parentheses identify the chapters in the textbook.

This hierarchy is also quite deep. While the first area, sources of law, has only one layer of categories, the next area, resolution of disputes, has three layers. Moving down to the classification of laws, we find two types, tort and contract. Tort has three categories, within which intentional tort has nine classifications and strict liability has three. On the contract side, only two types exist, but the formation of a contract—the conditions under which an "understanding" is a contract—is of much greater interest and importance.

Designing Your Own Graphic Syllabus

To design your own graphic syllabus, you should first consider the overall structure of your course. You have seen examples of five kinds of structure— debate/competition (with possible complementarity), parallelism, process, sequence/chronology, and categorical hierarchy—but these are not exhaustive.

Figure 3.14

Graphic Syllabus of CME 302: Phase Equilibria,
Dr. Robert W. Schwartz, 2000.
Type of Organization: Categorical Hierarchy (one layer)

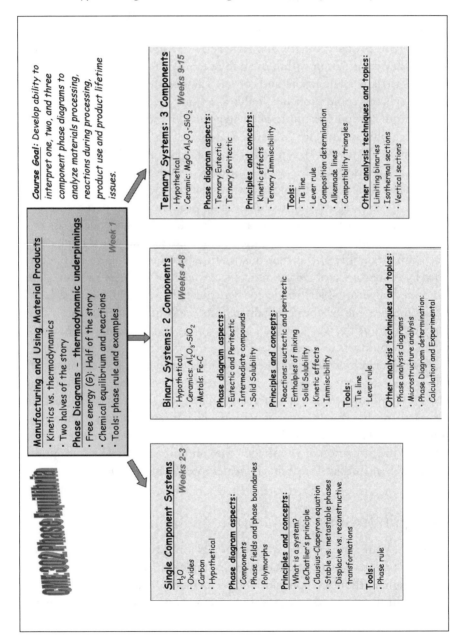

Figure 3.15

Graphic Syllabus of ME 404: Manufacturing Processes and Their Application,
Dr. Laine Mears, 2006.
Type of Organization: Categorical Hierarchy (multiple layers)

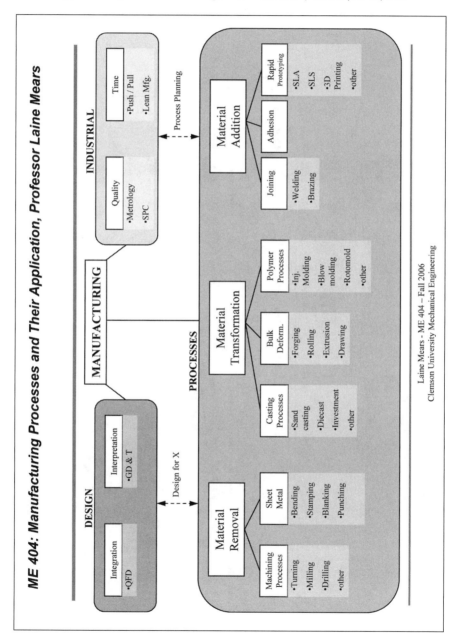

Figure 3.16

Graphic Syllabus of BLAW 280: Business Law I,
Dr. Carol Docan, 2006.
Type of Organization: Categorical Hierarchy (multiple layers)

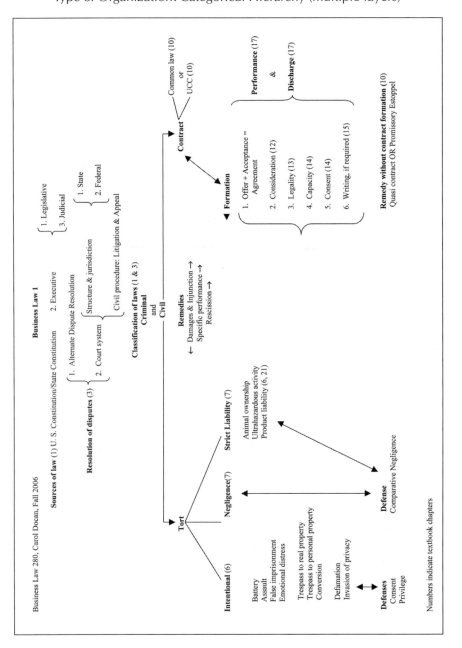

The additional examples of graphic syllabi in Appendix A show that a course, like a book, can follow many possible logics.

Let's assume for now that you already have a text syllabus, which means that you have already given your course an organization. It may or may not fall under one of the five structures. Or it may follow one structure in one or two segments of the course but not in all of it. The key question for you to answer is how *you* see your course in your mind. In that mental picture you can often detect one or more kinds of structure that give your course some order. You can resurrect what you had in mind while you were putting the course and its schedule of topics together. However, you may recall that you selected and ordered the topics to conform to the textbook. If the organization isn't yours and doesn't make sense, consider how difficult it must be for your students to structure and store the course material. If knowledge is not structured, it isn't retained. So it may be best to reorganize the course yourself.

If you are approaching a course fresh, without a preexisting structure, you can ask yourself how you see the field, subspecialty, or subject matter in your mind. How do you remember the knowledge within it? You must have a structure for that knowledge, or it wouldn't be in your mind at all. Does any part of that structure resemble any of the five types addressed in this chapter?

Once you determine the general structure of the course, you have several layout and graphic decisions to make. To start, the "direction" of the overall layout—that is, where the course starts and where it ends—may be down from the top (most common), up from the bottom (building up from a foundation), left to right, right to left, along a diagonal, or some combination of these options. For instance, both of Dr. Ebin's graphic syllabi (Figures 3.8 and 3.10) change directions, but her arrows make these shifts easy to follow.

You also have to decide how to arrange the information spatially, both overall and in specific areas of the graphic, which involves choices about the shapes of the enclosures. Figure 3.17 displays seven different spatial arrangements for a small amount of information (four strategies to get students to do the readings), and these do not exhaust the possibilities. The enclosures also vary, and some motifs don't even use them. Enclosures may take on any geometric, "auto shape," or drawn shape—you have seen a wide variety used in the graphic syllabi displayed in this chapter. While rectangles predominate, Dr. Ebin uses a tetrahedron, a six-sided figure, and an eight-sided figure in her graphic syllabus of HSCI 592: Advanced Biostatistics for the Health Sciences (Figure 3.10). Dr. Coffee's graphic syllabus of FDSC 215: Culinary Techniques (Figure 3.12) features exceptionally creative and fitting enclosures: the course name in a coffee cup (taking off on her last name), safety and sanitation topics in a stop sign; basic cooking topics in a cylinder suggesting a food bin, plate presentation topics in a plate-like figure, and the "course menu" in a rectangle that resembles a menu. The enclosures themselves serve the purpose of icons that help carry the verbal message. A hexagon signals caution, and given the shape of a question mark, triangles are prime spaces for inserting questions.

A few graphic syllabi also use shading or color to define groups of related topics or to set off tests and assignments from topics, for example Dr.. Spitler's HLTH 380: Epidemiology in Figure 3.7. Of course, color is not evident in this book, but if Dr. Spitler's syllabus is in your imagination, you might con-

Figure 3.17 (page 1)

Variations of Graphic Arrangements of Information

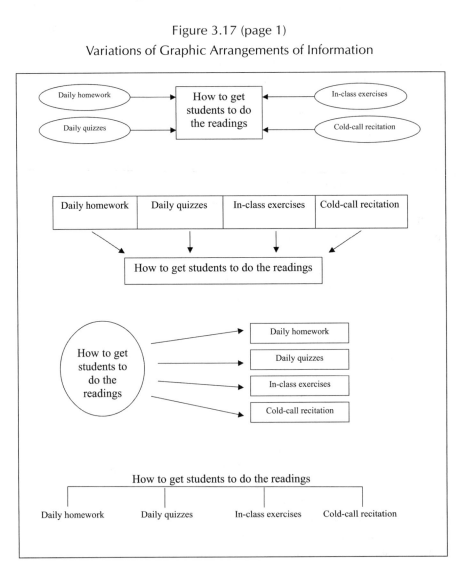

sider varying the colors of the enclosures and even the connecting lines and arrows. Borders around enclosures are yet another way to differentiate key topics from others.

Variations in type can also help distinguish major topics from subordinate ones. Most of the graphic syllabi shown here do this by varying type sizes and styles (bold, italics, underlining) and by inserting standard word processing graphics. None of these graphic syllabi use different fonts, but this is an option. Similarly, more important connecting lines may be thicker than others and less important lines, broken or dotted.

Figure 3.17 (page 2)

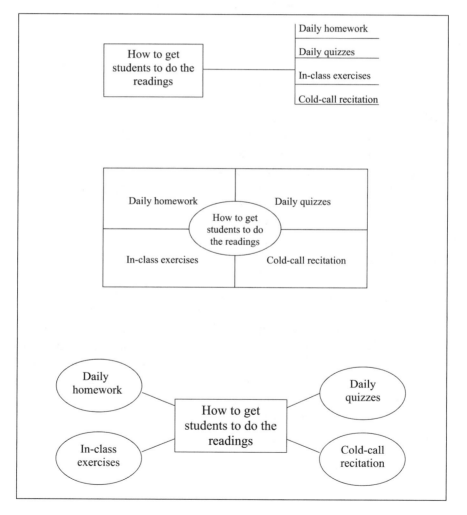

However, simplicity should override glitz and variety. After all, a graphic syllabus is a tool to *clarify* the organization of a course. Ideally, the syllabus fits on one page and presents a "map" that is clear enough for a total novice in the subject matter to follow. Clutter and complexity only subvert the purpose of the syllabus. This also means it should flow along one predominant "line" that moves through time, just as a course moves through the semester. Two-directional and double recursive arrows may be appropriate to show the actual relationship between concepts or variables, but they are best used sparingly to prevent students from losing their sense of direction. After all, a graphic syllabus represents the *flow of a course,* which is not necessarily the structure of the discipline and specialized area. A graphic that does depict the structure or history of a discipline may be a powerful learning aid for students, but it shouldn't be called a graphic "syllabus."

Graphic Metaphors

A graphic metaphor is a type of graphic syllabus that has an overall design or layout based on an object or set of objects. The object (or set of objects) need not be related to the subject matter of the course, but the metaphor is especially memorable when it is. A metaphor adds value by providing a single symbol of the course structure that facilitates and strengthens students' retention of the course material.

My graphic syllabus of the Free Will and Determinism seminar (Figure 3.13) is a very simple graphic metaphor that uses the object of umbrellas. The primary purpose of the umbrellas is to reinforce the relationships between the major philosophical schools of thought and the related readings. The large umbrella at the top indicates that the entire course, while cross-disciplinary, falls under the general "umbrella" of philosophy, as the metaphysical debate encompassing free agency, deliberation, voluntary behavior, and other underlying issues takes place in that discipline. This debate is the subject of the first few weeks of readings.

Directly under the philosophy umbrella are the major schools of thought, each of which has its own smaller umbrella with the related readings falling under it. Because fatalism does not explain how or why things happen, it has not spawned scientific studies, utopian extrapolations, or clinical approaches to read about. But it has a popular stepchild, a belief in spiritual destiny, for which there *are* readings, such as James Redfield's book, *The Celestine Prophecy.* The umbrella metaphor can easily be adapted to other courses organized around different theoretical perspectives or schools of thought. For instance, it would have suited my Social Stratification course (Figure 3.3).

The second graphic metaphor (see Figure 3.18) was designed by Dr. Joanna Penner for her 2004 course, Nursing Foundations, at Lethbridge Community

College in Alberta, Canada. She arranged her topics on a floor plan, with the course following the arrowed lines from one "room" to another. The floor plan does not resemble the standard layout of a house or office building, but that's because she chose to situate the "rooms" under four major topics (across the top row) to help her students understand the underlying organization of her course. Of course, the floor plan metaphor restricts the enclosures to room-like shapes with cutout doors, which, incidentally, standard software cannot draw.

Figure 3.18
Graphic Metaphor of Nursing 170: Nursing Foundations,
Dr. Joanne Penner, 2004

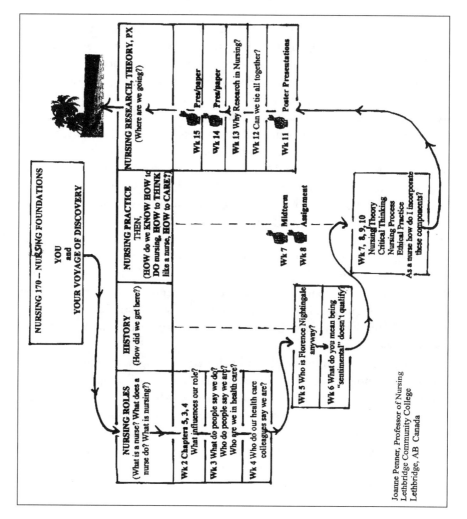

In the following three examples, the graphic metaphor is related to the subject matter of the course. Dr. A. Darlene Panvini, now associate professor of biology at Belmont University, designed the graphic in Figure 3.19 for the freshman seminar Conservation Ecology, which she taught at Vanderbilt University. As the graphic shows, the course has three major sections—Understanding Biodiversity, Losing Biodiversity, and Saving Biodiversity—each of which features one or two case studies and one or two major papers (shown in shaded boxes). Dr. Panvini intended her graphic to be only a graphic syllabus, but its elaborate web-like design makes it look organic, like an ecological system.

The third graphic metaphor (see Figure 3.20) was designed by Dr. Clarence A. Balch, a lecturer in the general engineering program at Clemson University, for his Engineering Graphics course. Strikingly drawn in three dimensions, its metaphorical objects are, in fact, engineering graphics, and Dr. Balch created them using engineering graphics software. The graphics elegantly mirror the subject matter of the course, and the spatial arrangement of the topics reflects the substantive relationships among them. The only problem with the graphic is its lack of flow through time, as topics in neighboring weeks are sometimes not adjacent or otherwise connected.

The final example (see Figure 3.21) was sketched by Dr. Robert Littleson, a lecturer in accountancy and legal studies at Clemson University, for his accounting course, Budgeting and Executive Control. Whimsically hand drawn, it depicts two buildings at a corporate site: a production facility, where the activity-based costing takes place, and an office building symbolizing management, where the activity-based and functional-based decision-making take place. The major course (and chapter) topics identify the various icons in the scene—the garbage heap, the workers, the smoke from the smoke stack, the bag of money, the incoming truck, and the sun—and the links between production and management. The circled numbers denote the relevant textbook chapters. The sequence of course topics through the semester is not clear from the graphic, but what is very clear is how the topics interrelate in corporate accounting operations.

Unless you are familiar with sophisticated drawing or design software, a graphic metaphor can be much more difficult than a standard graphic syllabus to produce on the computer. For instance, neither Microsoft Word nor PowerPoint will allow you to draw boxes with the openings for doors that are necessary for the floor-plan metaphor. You may have to turn to low-tech alternatives, such as pens, pencils, markers, crayons, rulers, triangles, T-squares, compasses, cutouts, and tracing paper. If you need a digitized version, you can always scan your hand-drawing or email it to yourself using a digital sender.

Figure 3.19

Graphic Metaphor of Freshman Seminar: Conservation Ecology,
Dr. A. Darlene Panvini, 1996

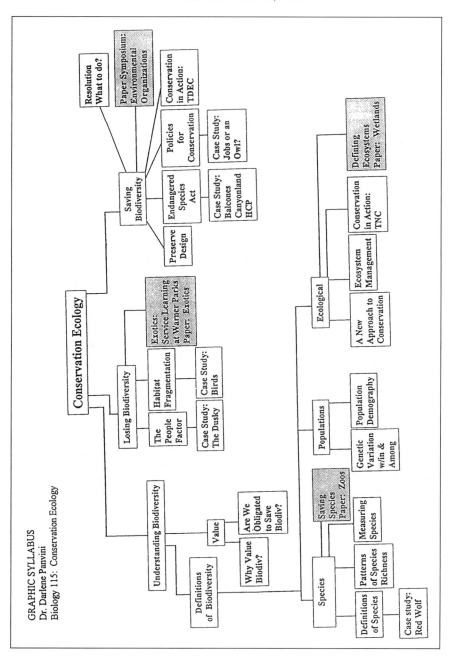

Figure 3.20

Graphic Metaphor of EG 209: Engineering Graphics,
Dr. Clarence Balch, 2000

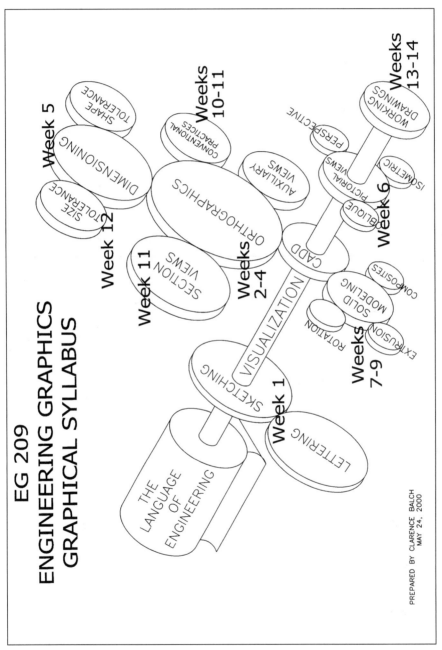

Figure 3.21
Graphic Metaphor of ACCT 410: Budgeting and Executive Control,
Dr. Robert Littleson, 2000

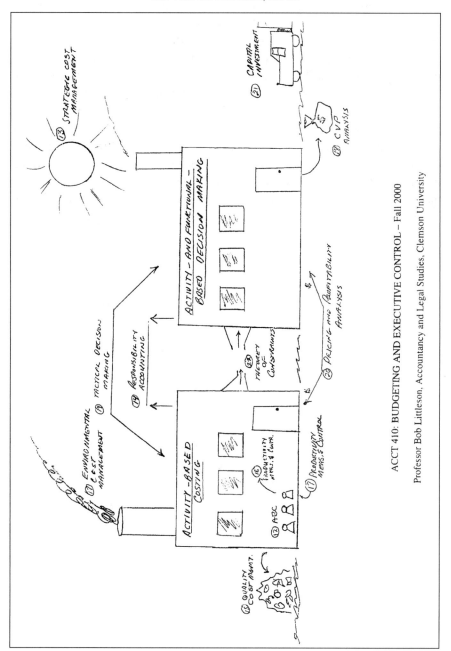

What Students Care About

In the final analysis, even students of the Net Generation are not likely to care whether a helpful learning tool is computer-produced or, if you draw it yourself, whether it is artistic. What they and every other generation of students have cared about is how much you care about them as people and as learners. Going the extra mile to create a graphic syllabus that helps them understand the course structure and the material more easily is what will impress them. Making them smile in the process helps their learning even more.

Dr. Ebin, the associate professor of health education at Cal State Northridge, who contributed two graphic syllabi to this book, recently surveyed her Advanced Biostatistics students to obtain their assessment of her "course conceptual framework" (graphic syllabus). Their written comments included these: "It really helped to see a visual of the syllabus." "This course is so scary that anything helps." "I like having the dates on the graphic." "I am a visual learner." "I like pictures." Indeed, students appreciate our gestures to help them learn.

4

Charting an Outcomes Map

An outcomes map is a flowchart of the student learning objectives of a course. It shows the sequence and progression of the skills and abilities that students should be able to demonstrate at various times in the semester.

This flowchart idea may sound alien in the context of student learning objectives or outcomes because we are used to thinking of them in a list. Accrediting agencies recommend or require that all courses have such a list in their text syllabi, and a few instructors voluntarily supply a list for each major unit of their courses. These lists usually specify what students should be able to do by the end of the course or unit, and perhaps a few of the skills and abilities they should acquire along the way. But a list gives students no idea of the preparation needed to meet the course objectives.

Ideally, a course is designed to build up students' readiness to meet a logical succession of learning objectives. To achieve one objective in the middle or the end of a course, a student must typically meet one or more other objectives earlier in the semester. If he or she cannot meet the prerequisite objectives, the student won't be able to meet the latter ones. For instance, if students are supposed to be able to develop a research proposal at some point in the course, they will have to be able do a number of other things beforehand: frame a research problem or hypothesis, argue its importance, conduct and write a literature review, devise an appropriate research design (and all that this involves), plan the data collection and analysis (which assumes some methodological expertise), explain the impact of the study's expected findings, and develop a mock budget. Developing a research proposal, then, requires a collection of rather sophisticated skills. If the course or prerequisite courses fail to provide learning and practice opportunities in these skills, the students are doomed to produce substandard proposals. Or the instructor will have to dilute the standards for an acceptable end product.

Designing a course as a progression of outcomes only makes sense, and yet this kind of reasoning is more the exception than the rule. Creating an outcomes map as part of the course design process fosters this kind of reasoning. It also displays the reasoning for students to see and follow.

Developing Student Learning Objectives

Before laying out strategies for designing a course or an outcomes map, let's clarify the meaning and nature of a sound student learning objective (or outcome). It is *not* a description of the course content or what you intend to teach. Instead, it is a statement of what your students should be able to *do* by a certain time in a course. Such a promise presumes that your students fulfill their end of the learning process—that is, attend class regularly, take good notes on lectures, participate actively in all in-class activities, dutifully do the readings and any other homework assignments, study adequately for exams, and meet any other learning requirements you set. As advised in Chapter 1, you should make these conditions explicit in your text syllabus. Such a promise also presumes that you as the instructor design, implement, and assess, with feedback, the assignments and in-class activities that will give students appropriate and sufficient opportunities to gain the knowledge, skills, and practice they need to meet the learning objective.

The *do* focus of an objective accomplishes much more than meeting the accountability requirements of accrediting agencies. To begin with, it helps ensure learning in two ways. First, it specifies an action that students should be able to perform. If they can do nothing with knowledge, not even recognize and regurgitate it, they haven't learned a thing. Second, *doing* implies an activity, which means students can learn how to do it only by being active, which means attempting and practicing the activity.

Yet another important purpose of the *do* emphasis is to make the learning observable and therefore assessable. As the instructor, you should be able to see or hear or otherwise sense—taste and smell, if your area is food science or culinary arts—your students' demonstration of their learning. If you can't perceive it, you can't measure it, so you can't assess and grade it. That is the problem with learning objectives that use verbs that reflect internal states—for example, to *know,* to *understand,* to *learn,* to *feel,* to *appreciate.* How can you tell what your students know if what they know is only in their heads? They have to *show* that knowledge by doing something with it.

Specify the conditions or context for the performance, if these are not obvious. You might want your students to be able to explain and defend their position on something in writing, orally, or in both forms (such as a paper followed by a colloquium or debate). You might want them to be able to interview a patient while manifesting sensitivity to that individual's cultural norms and values, but the context may be in a role-play, a clinical setting, a written script, or a multimedia presentation.

One final benefit of the focus on *doing* is that you specify exactly how you want your students to learn certain material, so they know how to study correctly and efficiently. If you tell your students you want them to be able to *recognize* the definitions of a list of terms, they will study for that cognitive operation, perhaps with flash cards or a matching-type review. This style of studying is quite different from studying to *reproduce*. If you ask students to *define* a list of terms, they will probably spend their time memorizing definitions. (When you are tempted to declare that you want your students to *know, learn,* or *understand* something, ask yourself what you will want them to do to *show* they have met your objective.) If you say you will ask them to analyze and evaluate a theory or perspective, they will study it in a much more critical, analytical way than if you tell them they will have to describe or summarize it.

Before you begin writing student learning objectives for a course you haven't taught before, do a little research. Ask your department chair or dean whether an accrediting agency has already mandated a list of objectives. For instance, the National Council for the Accreditation of Teacher Education mandates objectives for many education courses, and the Accreditation Board for Engineering specifies program objectives, some of which may be targeted to your course. Also find out about the history of the course—in particular, why it was developed and what special learning purposes it was designed to serve (Prégent, 1994). Your course may occupy a key niche in the curriculum that you will be responsible for filling. Finally, familiarize yourself with the students most likely to take the course. What are their year(s) in college, their intended or actual majors, their reasons for taking the course, their backgrounds and abilities in the subject matter, and their expectations of the course? Depending on the course, such information may be available from your institution's admissions office, student affairs office, or career center, but your colleagues, especially those who have taught the course before, are probably your most valuable source of information. They will be able to tell you the "cognitive demographics" of the typical students and how well certain subjects, books, teaching methods, activities, and assignments have worked in the course.

Course Design by Objectives

Your student learning objectives are the skeletal framework for your course. You will certainly have *cognitive* objectives, as all college-level courses aim to develop thinking skills. This section will focus mainly on these. But you may also want your students to acquire *psychomotor* (physical action) skills if your discipline is in the arts, health or laboratory sciences, linguistics, or foreign languages. You may have *affective* objectives if your field of practice requires open-mindedness, empathy, and/or an appreciation of diversity, as do clinical psychology, counseling, pastoral studies, management, and the health fields. If developing your students' collaborative and teamwork abilities is important in your course, whatever your discipline, you may have *social* objectives. Last but not least are *ethical* objectives, which have taken on new significance as universities attempt to counter well-publicized ethical lapses in the greater society. In many institutions, courses are designed to teach students to integrate moral considerations into their future occupational decision-making, especially in the fields of business, health, law, education, engineering, and the sciences.

Whatever your learning objectives, all the assignments and in-class activities, including lectures, should help your students meet those objectives, and all the assessments, formal and informal, should be designed to measure your students' progress toward meeting those objectives. As previously explained, a course is a learning process of advancing through a logical succession of objectives. Some of the objectives must be met early in the semester to prepare students to meet more advanced objectives later in the course.

Ultimate Objectives

The easiest way to develop this logical succession is to formulate your end-of-semester, or *ultimate,* student learning objectives first. These are likely to be the most challenging skills and cognitively complex tasks you intend your students to master. They probably demand high levels of thinking (e.g., analysis and evaluation) and problem solving and require students to not only use but to integrate several abilities they have acquired during the course. It normally takes a major capstone assignment or a comprehensive final, or both, to assess how well students have met these objectives.

Mediating Objectives

From here you work backwards, determining what skills and tasks your students will have to demonstrate and perform before they can achieve your ultimate objectives. These are your *mediating* objectives, and you will probably have quite a few of them, each representing a component or lower level of your ultimate objectives. Your challenge now is to determine the most logical and efficient order in which students should acquire these mediating abilities.

In the example at the beginning of this chapter, the ultimate objective was to write a research proposal, which requires that students first learn how to frame a research problem or hypothesis, then to argue its importance, then to conduct and write a literature review, then to devise an appropriate research design, then to plan the data collection and analysis, then to explain the impact of the study's expected findings, and finally to develop a mock budget. Such a sequence of tasks describes an established process. In cumulative subjects such as mathematics, physics, and engineering, the order of objectives also follows a skill-building logic.

However, many courses allow the instructor a lot of discretionary room for sequencing objectives, in which case this aspect of teaching becomes an art. Textbooks might prescribe a certain order, but much of it may be arbitrary. Consider introductory survey courses, literature courses, even certain science and nursing courses. Both the topics students study and the skills they should acquire may be ordered in different ways. Generally the less lock-step the curriculum, the more discretion instructors have in sequencing the mediating objectives in their courses.

Foundational Objectives

Once you work your way back to the beginning of the course, you delineate your *foundational* learning objectives. These may involve relatively low-order cognitive operations, such as being able to recognize or paraphrase technical definitions, recall basic facts, define concepts, and summarize theoretical frameworks. After all, students can't interpret, utilize, interrelate, assess, or create knowledge when they cannot speak or write the language of the discipline. In fact, foundational objectives may assume importance at other junctures in the course if it is organized into different modules of knowledge. In this case, students may have to master a whole new set of terms, concepts, theories, and basic facts several times during the semester.

Your foundational objectives may involve much higher level cognitive processes, such as major shifts in the students' way of looking at some aspect of reality. Your task—and it's a challenging one—is to create learning situations in which they recognize that their mental model or paradigm is faulty and the one the discipline offers is superior. Whatever model they take through the course is the structure into which they will attempt to incorporate and store any new knowledge on the subject. As we saw in Chapters 1 and 2, ensuring that students have the discipline's model in their minds is critical to their learning anything else. If they have the wrong model, it will not accommodate the new knowledge and abilities you intend for them to learn. As a result, the students will not be able to learn them, at least not at a deep level.

For example, to master physics on a serious level, the learner must replace his or her Aristotelian or Newtonian model of the physical world, either of which "work" for us in everyday life, with Einstein's model. To think like a sociologist, a student must abandon the individualistic free-will explanation for the situations in which people find themselves and embrace the deterministic, probabilistic view that the social structure stacks the deck in favor or against people attaining certain situations, and that one's location in the social structure at birth is the strongest single determinant. To grasp evolutionary biology, learners must reject the notion that Homo sapiens represent the ultimate "destination" of epochs of evolving complexity and adaptation and instead view our species as just another temporarily successful branch among millions of others.

Moreover, to begin to comprehend *any* body of knowledge, students must acquire an understanding of what knowledge is and what it isn't. Almost all students come to us with the misconceived notion of knowledge as "information"—that is, a huge collection of immutable terms and loosely related facts that we are supposed to transmit and they are supposed to memorize. Perry (1968) called this faulty mental model "dualism." This is the first misconception we should discredit before escorting students into our subject matter. We must guide them in discovering that our disciplines are inherently full of uncertainties and unknowns, and not because we just haven't gotten around to "filling in all the blanks." Rather, these uncertainties and unknowns belie a reality that is not always systematic. Knowledge is simply a "grid" that human beings have created and imposed over this "messy" reality to try to "tame" and manipulate it. This grid encompasses all the patterns we have identified through our observations, along with our best-evidenced interpretations of them at this point in time (Kuhn, 1970). Once students abandon their comfortable black-and-white view of reality, their minds can broaden into relativism and, if we help them learn to evaluate competing perspectives critically, they will come around to favoring the more valid mental models (Perry, 1968).

Helpful Frameworks for Designing a Course

The literatures on cognitive operations, undergraduate cognitive development, and course design suggest logical ways to sequence learning outcomes. Five frameworks—Bloom's (1956), Anderson and Krathwohl's (2000), Perry's (1968), Baxter Magolda's (1992), and Fink's (2003)—are offered to you to consider using as the scaffolding of your course. You may select one schema or draw on one or more of them as heuristic devices.

Bloom's Framework

Perhaps the oldest and most familiar framework is Bloom's (1956) hierarchical taxonomy of cognitive operations. It posits that students must be able to perform one or more thinking tasks before they can learn to perform another. In this hierarchy, the most basic operation is *knowledge,* which is the ability to recall and either restate or recognize material. Having knowledge enables the student to gain *comprehension* of that material, which is the ability to paraphrase it in one's own words. Learners who have mastered these two operations are prepared to tackle *application,* which means using that material in new, concrete situations, to include identifying appropriate examples. Only after learning to apply material can a student learn to conduct an *analysis* of it—that is, to discern and examine its structure and discriminate among its component parts. With this ability mastered, he or she can proceed to *synthesis,* the ability to rearrange elements of the material so as to design, compose, construct, or predict something original from it. The most advanced cognitive operation, according to Bloom, is *evaluation*—the ability to assess, support, or challenge the material—which requires facility in all the previous cognitive skills.

Students must be able to define certain concepts, state certain principles, and recall certain facts, as well as paraphrase them, before thinking about them more complexly. But beyond that, Bloom's sequencing breaks down. For example, in the professions (e.g., law, medicine, the ministry), the highest order cognitive operation is the application of disciplinary knowledge to new, often complicated situations. Deciding what knowledge is relevant and how to apply it involves analyzing the elements of the "fuzzy" problematic situation, evaluating the utility of the disciplinary algorithms to the situation, and synthesizing a legal strategy, medical diagnosis and treatment, or moral/theological resolution. For another illustration, designing a research study is a synthetic project, according to Bloom, but doesn't it also demand, at the very least, evaluation of the research question, the existing literature, and the methodological alternatives?

Anderson and Krathwohl's Framework

A more user-friendly, updated framework is Anderson and Krathwohl's (2000) revision of Bloom's taxonomy. It translates the sometimes awkward nouns for the cognitive operations into verbs—for example, replacing "knowledge" with the more appropriate *remember,* and not only substituting "synthesis" with *create* but also elevating it to the top rung. In between these, the verbs are sequenced as follows: *understanding, applying, analyzing,* and *evaluating.* This order, with *creating* designated the most advanced level of thinking, makes more intuitive sense than Bloom's, yet the strict hierarchy does not accommodate the sophisticated kind of application required in the professions. Still, Anderson and Krathwohl make a major contribution in crossing their taxonomy with levels of knowledge: factual, conceptual, procedural, and metacognitive. The four levels create a robust and intuitively appealing hierarchy that reveals the complexities of the cognitive operations they intersect.

Perry's Framework

Perry's (1968) cognitive theory of undergraduate development presents another sequenced framework for course design, although it doesn't easily transfer to many undergraduate courses. His first stage of development, dualism, was mentioned earlier in the section on foundational objectives as a hindrance to students being able to learn new knowledge. Therefore, prying them away from this comfortable black-and-white view of reality might be a necessary first task for some instructors. Each of Perry's stages is distinguished by how the student explains or interprets uncertainty in knowledge:

1. Duality: Uncertainty doesn't exist. Authorities know all of what is true.

2. Multiplicity a): Uncertainty is due to incompetent authorities (or the instructor is merely leading students through an intellectual exercise).

3. Multiplicity b): Uncertainty exists because authorities haven't gotten around to answering the questions.

4. Relativism a): Uncertainty is inherent and pervasive. Since there is no certainty, all knowledge is opinion and all opinions are equally valid.

5. Relativism b): Uncertainty pervades some areas but not all—for example, not the purely factual.

6. Commitment a): Uncertainty deters action, but action must be taken. Relativism fails to supply answers to living in the world, so commitment may be necessary.

7. Commitment b): An initial, tentative commitment is made to the viewpoint that knowledge and ethics are developed from experience and learning, then integrated into a consistent philosophy.

8. Commitment c): The implications and trade-offs of commitment are realized and accepted.

9. Commitment d): Adjusting and even changing commitments are integral to the lifelong pursuit of personal growth and wisdom.

The less detailed version of this framework includes just four major stages: dualism, multiplicity, relativism, and commitment.

To design a course to follow Perry's stages, sequence your student learning objectives to reflect their progress through each of the developmental stages, whether nine or four, or at least through relativism. Therefore, an early objective would expect students to acknowledge that certainty indeed exists and authorities don't have all the answers. A mediating objective would have students being able to explain and critique multiple competing viewpoints. To meet an ultimate objective, a student would have to adopt one of the viewpoints, justify his or her choice, and qualify it, explicating the limitations of the chosen viewpoint. While Perry's framework may have little to offer an undergraduate science or engineering course, it can prove very useful in interpretive disciplines such as literature, the arts, and philosophy.

Baxter Magolda's Framework

To correct for the fact that Perry crafted and tested his schema only on undergraduate males, Baxter Magolda (1992) studied both males and females and developed four levels of knowing—absolute, transitional, independent, and contextual. Her levels roughly parallel Perry's simplified version, but she also discovered that females tend to follow a "relational" pattern and that males tend to follow an "abstract" pattern.

Fink's Framework

While Bloom's, Anderson and Krathwohl's, Perry's, and Baxter Magolda's taxonomies propose a built-in sequencing of outcomes, Fink's (2003) categories of learning do not. Although he does posit *foundational knowledge* (recalling and understanding ideas and information) as the basis for most other kinds of learning, his approach, instead of being hierarchical, is cumulative and interactive. Beyond foundational knowledge, Fink proposes five additional categories of learning:

- *Application,* in which students engage in any combination of critical, practical, and creative thinking, acquire key skills, and learn how to manage complex projects, all for the purpose of making other kinds of learning useful

- *Integration,* in which students perceive connections among ideas, disciplines, people, and realms of their lives

- *Human dimension,* in which students gain a new understanding of themselves and/or others, often by seeing the human implications of other kinds of learning

- *Caring,* an affective outcome, in which students acquire new interests, feelings, and/or values about what they are learning and, in turn, are motivated to learn more about it

- *Learning how to learn,* in which students learn about the process of their particular learning and learning in general, such that they can pursue learning more self-consciously, efficiently, and effectively

The challenge for the instructor is not to order these kinds of learning but to help students interrelate and engage in them synergistically (Fink, 2003). For example, if you put students in a situation where they can apply new knowledge to solve a problem of relevance to them (application) or where they can see how some phenomenon impacts them and others (human dimension), they will probably become more interested in the knowledge (caring). As their interest grows, they are more likely to notice its relationships to other things they have learned (integration). As they make more connections, they may perceive more implications for their own and others' lives (human dimension) and may come to see greater utility in the knowledge to improve the quality of life (application). At this point, they may want to learn still more (caring) while realizing that they need to acquire stronger learning skills (learning how to learn) to do so. This is only one illustration of the way that a positive learning and motivation spiral can take off and continue to ascend.

According to Fink, an ideally designed and developed course promotes all six kinds of learning, resulting in a genuinely "significant" learning experience. An outcomes map based on Fink's framework might start with foundational knowledge but would progressively add objectives that reflect the other five kinds of learning. Different kinds of learning may enter into the course several times during the semester. The idea is to bring all six kinds into the students' learning process by the end of the course. In his book, Fink supports his contention that this goal is possible for just about any course, even an online course, by furnishing a comprehensive, step-by-step procedure for reaching the goal.

Examples of Outcomes Maps

An outcomes map is simply a visual representation of your course design by objectives. It displays the sequence, progression, and accumulation of the skills and abilities that students should be able to demonstrate through the semester—that is, the order of and interrelationships among your student outcomes. In particular, it shows how meeting one or more objectives enables the student to meet subsequent objectives. In other words, it flowcharts the learning process that you as the instructor have charted for your students.

It may sound as though an outcomes map allows less room for variation and creativity than a graphic syllabus, but the examples included here call that supposition into question. Like graphic syllabi, these maps move in different directions and combinations of directions. They use a variety of spatial arrangements, enclosures, connectors, type sizes, type styles, and shadings. They reflect the influence of different course design frameworks. Some outcomes maps are more detailed than others. Some supply the week or class number of each learning objective while others do not. But they all furnish students with far more information about how their learning will progress through the course than a simple, linear list of objectives ever can.

Let's take the issue of variety one step further by examining three outcomes maps that were designed by three different instructors during roughly the same time period. The outcomes maps were for the same course, MGT 312: Decision Models for Management, at the same university (Clemson). Because this is a required junior-level course in the management major, its content and student outcomes are largely defined by the department, yet the instructors produced markedly different graphics (see Figures 4.1, 4.2, 4.3). Still, the more closely you read the instructors' texts, the more similarities you will find. If you compare Uzay Damali's outcomes map (Figure 4.1) with Hua-Hung (Robin) Weng's (Figure 4.2) and can match up the class periods by number, you will notice that in both cases Classes 3 to 8 concentrate on expressing and solving management problems using LP models, Classes 11 and 12 focus on employing a sensitivity report, and Classes 14 to 17 address solving network and integer problems. Other such overlaps are also evident. While Mohammed Raja's outcomes map (Figure 4.3) lacks time-in-semester benchmarks, you can see that the flow of learning objectives follows much the same plan.

All three outcomes maps, especially Mr. Damali's and Mr. Raja's, display the general influence of Bloom's taxonomy. Early in the course, student outcomes focus on defining, identifying, describing, explaining, and operating software in routine ways. A few weeks into the course, they advance to applying and solving, then analyzing, constructing/developing a model, and evaluating different approaches to a problem.

This progression of learning objectives is evident in other examples as well, such as Samuel Otim's outcomes map of MGT 490: Strategic Management of Information Technology (see Figure 4.4). However, Mr. Otim does not strictly follow Bloom's schema. While his Module I outcomes are all on

Figure 4.1

Outcomes Map of MGT 312: Decision Models for Management,
Uzay Damali, 2007

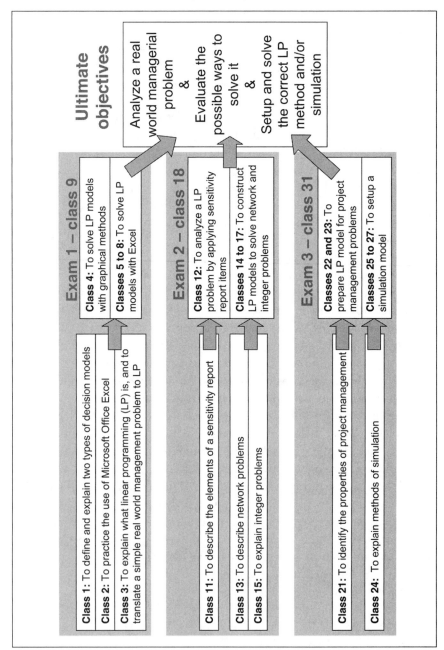

Figure 4.2

Outcomes Map of MGT 312: Decision Models for Management,
Hua-Hung (Robin) Weng, 2006

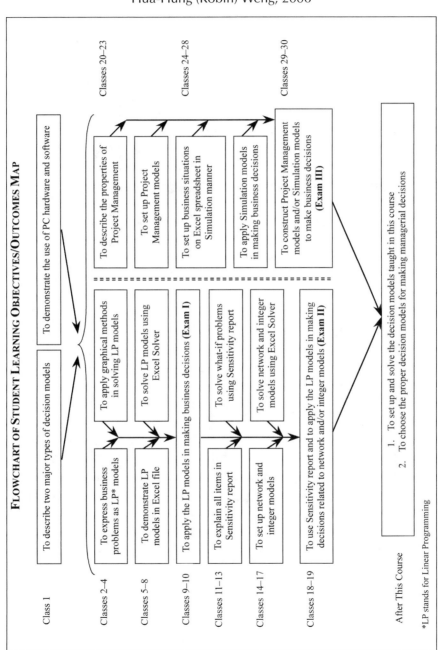

Figure 4.3

Outcomes Map of MGT 312: Decision Models for Management
(AKA Managerial Decision Modeling),
Mohammed Raja, 2006

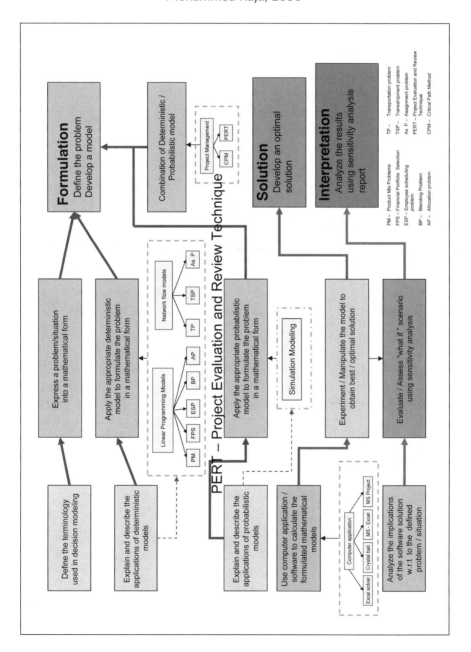

the knowledge/comprehension level, those in Module II are on that level plus application and evaluation, and those in Module III involve synthesis and evaluation.

Leslie Moreland does not strictly apply Bloom's taxonomy in her outcomes map for PRTM 255: Sport Management for Intercollegiate Athletics (see Figure 4.5) either, but Bloom's influence is evident after the first few classes. Her course opens with an evaluation of intercollegiate athletics, which is a high-level cognitive operation. However, the students presumably come into this course knowing a great deal about intercollegiate athletics. Using what they know to assess the state of the industry provides an excellent springboard for learning how to manage events within it. Then the students begin to tackle knowledge objectives related to sport management and move up through higher order cognitive processes, ultimately using several such processes to "synthesize" an athletic event development plan. Ms. Moreland also includes in her map the key assignments and activities she uses to prepare students to meet each objective or to assess their performance on the objective (shown in parentheses within the map).

Irem Arsal's outcomes map of PRTM 391: E-Commerce and Tourism Marketing (see Figure 4.6) closely mirrors Anderson and Krathwohl's framework. Starting off with "remembering" ICT (information and communication technologies) terminology, Ms. Arsal then leads her students through understanding it, analyzing the implications of ITCs, recognizing real-world examples (applying), evaluating the Internet's effects on tourism sectors, and finally creating an online marketing plan.

The design of Dr. David O. Prevatt's graduate-level course, CE 809: Forensic Engineering, also reflects the Anderson and Krathwohl model. In his outcomes map (see Figure 4.7), most of what he calls the "basic skills" and even his mediating objectives seem to concentrate on remembering, understanding, and applying. His student assessment activities require applying and analyzing, and his "final" objectives focus on evaluating a forensic report, then "creating" a proposal, a report, and investigation plan for hypothetical incidents. The categories of his objectives/activities are color-coded in the original map.

My earliest outcomes map was for a unique, cross-disciplinary freshman seminar, Free Will and Determinism, which I taught at Vanderbilt University in the mid-1990s (see Figure 4.8). I developed it with the explicit purpose of leading students through all four of Perry's major stages of undergraduate development on an issue of interest to young college students: why things happen to people as they do in life. To meet my foundational objectives, which were to summarize all the major competing philosophies on the issue, including their assumptions and justifications, students presumably had to admit that the issue

Figure 4.4

Outcomes Map of MGT 490:
Strategic Management of Information Technology,
Samuel Otim, 2007

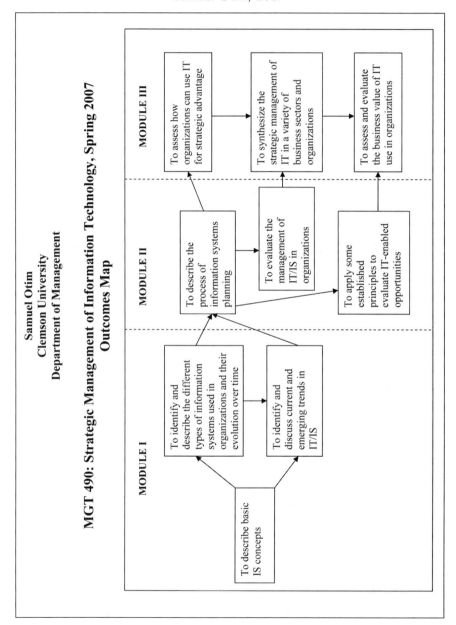

Figure 4.5

Outcomes Map for PRTM 255:
Sport Management for Intercollegiate Athletics,
Leslie Moreland, 2006

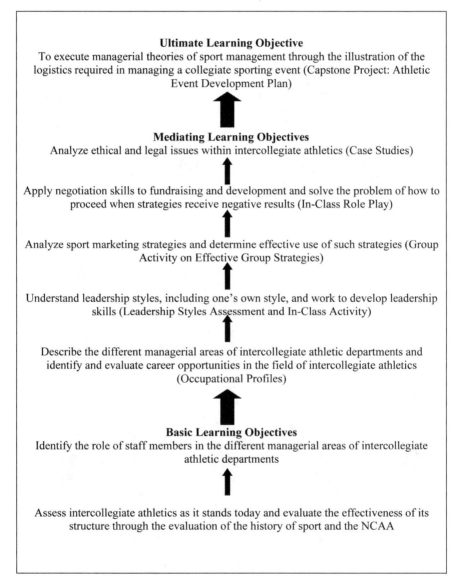

Ultimate Learning Objective
To execute managerial theories of sport management through the illustration of the
logistics required in managing a collegiate sporting event (Capstone Project: Athletic
Event Development Plan)

Mediating Learning Objectives
Analyze ethical and legal issues within intercollegiate athletics (Case Studies)

Apply negotiation skills to fundraising and development and solve the problem of how to
proceed when strategies receive negative results (In-Class Role Play)

Analyze sport marketing strategies and determine effective use of such strategies (Group
Activity on Effective Group Strategies)

Understand leadership styles, including one's own style, and work to develop leadership
skills (Leadership Styles Assessment and In-Class Activity)

Describe the different managerial areas of intercollegiate athletic departments and
identify and evaluate career opportunities in the field of intercollegiate athletics
(Occupational Profiles)

Basic Learning Objectives
Identify the role of staff members in the different managerial areas of intercollegiate
athletic departments

Assess intercollegiate athletics as it stands today and evaluate the effectiveness of its
structure through the evaluation of the history of sport and the NCAA

Figure 4.6

Outcomes Map of PRTM 391: E-Commerce and Tourism Marketing,
Irem Arsal, 2006

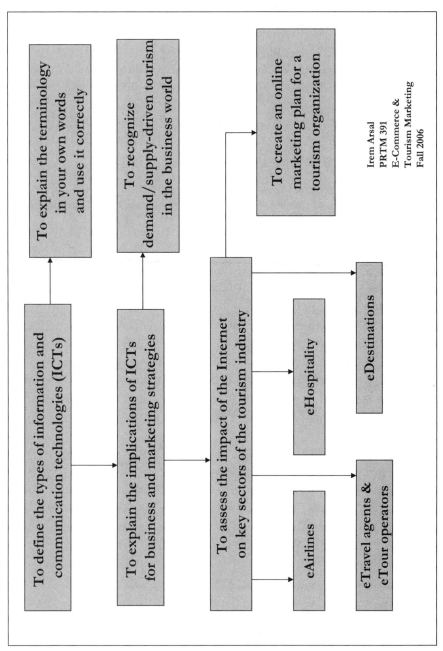

Figure 4.7
Outcomes Map of CE 809: Forensic Engineering,
Dr. David O. Prevatt, 2006

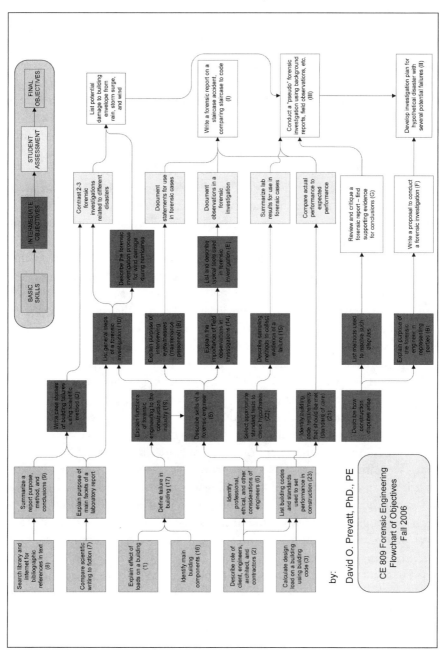

had no clear and certain explanation. If these assignments and activities didn't convince them that the uncertainty was inherent and pervasive, debating the philosophies when applied to a real-world criminal case hopefully would—and move them into relativism. Then students had to bring research from assigned readings and their own life experience to bear on evaluating each position's strengths and weaknesses. The intention here was to prevent their relativism from congealing, allowing them to discover that some positions had better evidence and/or more practical utility than others. Finally, to meet the course's ultimate learning objective, the students had to write a paper that made a tentative commitment to a personal position. They had to justify the position with logical, research-based reasoning, and, to reinforce its tentative nature, they had to acknowledge their position's limitations and weaknesses.

Under each objective in Figure 4.8 are the readings, written assignments, and in-class activities I selected or designed as the means to help students meet each objective. If the capstone papers are sufficient evidence, the course successfully helped students achieve a high level of intellectual maturity, at least as far as the central issue was concerned.

While Perry's stages provided the course scaffolding, the ordering and phraseology of the learning objectives also reflect Bloom's taxonomy and Anderson and Krathwohl's revision, which had not yet been published when I designed this course. From basic knowledge and comprehension of the taxonomy, students apply, then analyze, then evaluate the competing philosophies, and finally, create/synthesize and evaluate their own.

Figure 4.9 is the outcomes map I developed for my graduate-level course at Clemson University, VTED 876: College Teaching. It illustrates how Fink's categories of learning can interrelate and work synergistically in a course design. The course opens with considerable foundational knowledge about college students—developmental, cognitive, affective, and behavioral—which also brings in the human dimension. The graduate students often learn something about themselves as well as their future "audience" (their current audience if they are also employed as teaching assistants). For example, they find out about their own learning styles and add to their skills in learning how to learn. Since all of those who enroll in the course intend to teach at the college level after receiving their degrees, the topic of their own students should also evoke caring.

Then the graduate students have to begin the process of integrating and applying this foundational knowledge—first, in devising strategies to motivate their students, then in developing an undergraduate course of their choosing that incorporates both this "audience" awareness and these motivational strategies. The course design and development process, a series of steps

Figure 4.8

Outcomes Map of Freshman Seminar: Free Will and Determinism,
Dr. Linda B. Nilson, 1996

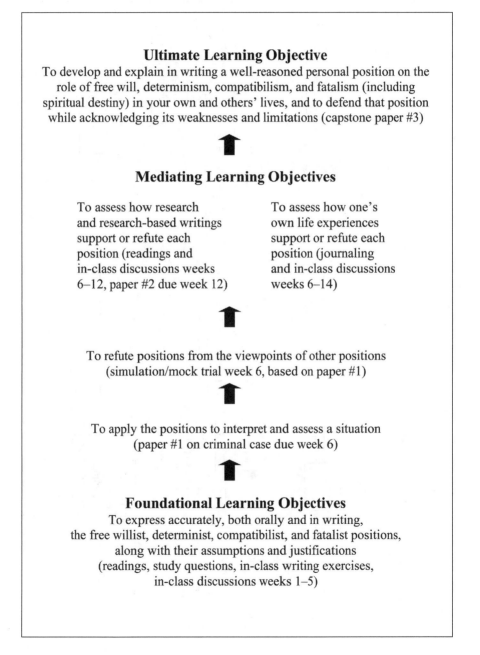

Ultimate Learning Objective

To develop and explain in writing a well-reasoned personal position on the
role of free will, determinism, compatibilism, and fatalism (including
spiritual destiny) in your own and others' lives, and to defend that position
while acknowledging its weaknesses and limitations (capstone paper #3)

Mediating Learning Objectives

To assess how research and research-based writings support or refute each position (readings and in-class discussions weeks 6–12, paper #2 due week 12)

To assess how one's own life experiences support or refute each position (journaling and in-class discussions weeks 6–14)

To refute positions from the viewpoints of other positions
(simulation/mock trial week 6, based on paper #1)

To apply the positions to interpret and assess a situation
(paper #1 on criminal case due week 6)

Foundational Learning Objectives

To express accurately, both orally and in writing,
the free willist, determinist, compatibilist, and fatalist positions,
along with their assumptions and justifications
(readings, study questions, in-class writing exercises,
in-class discussions weeks 1–5)

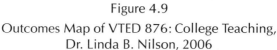

Figure 4.9

Outcomes Map of VTED 876: College Teaching,
Dr. Linda B. Nilson, 2006

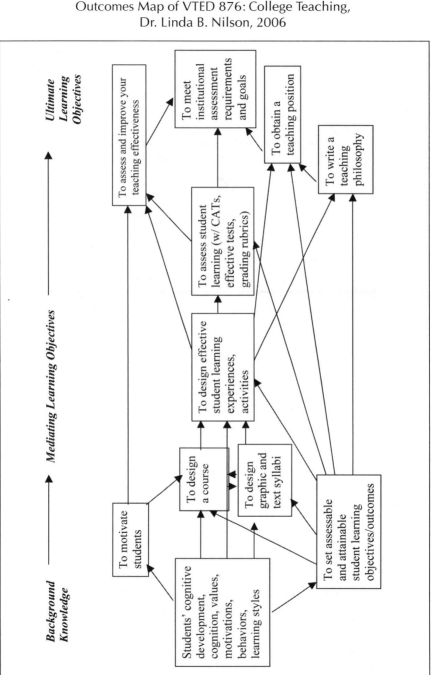

taking more than half the semester, involves additional foundational knowledge about learning objectives/outcomes, teaching techniques, and assessment methods. The graduate students must integrate and apply this knowledge in a course design that tightly links the ends (student learning objectives), the means (teaching strategies), and the methods for assessing students' progress toward the ends. Their culminating integrative assignment is writing a statement of their teaching philosophy that generates self-insight (human dimension) and helps the students prepare for the job market (caring).

The last couple of weeks focus on issues related to launching their career: writing a curriculum vitae, conducting an academic job search, applying for faculty positions, assembling evidence of teaching effectiveness, and academic job interviewing. These are practical application topics that the students invariably care a great deal about.

The last two examples of outcomes maps do not reflect any particular framework of cognitive processes, cognitive development, or course design, but both courses are perfectly logical and viable. T. Jefferson Shockley's outcomes map (see Figure 4.10) shows that his course, MGT 390: Introduction to Operations Management, is organized as a hierarchical sequence of modules. Each module addresses a list of learning objectives (left-hand boxes) at varying levels of cognitive complexity, from simple knowledge/remembering to application, analysis, and creation. Mastering the skills on each list "adds up to" meeting a broader objective (right-hand boxes), which in turn equips students to begin learning the skills in the next module.

Pamela S. Galluch's outcomes map (see Figure 4.11) also reflects the modular design of her course, MGT 318: Management Information Systems, but her three modules are more independent of each other. Each column of objectives in the shaded boxes culminates in a broader objective, which is the focus of the respective exam. Each exam addresses abilities that are only tangentially related to each other. However, Ms. Galluch's "ultimate learning objective" integrates all three modules, and students are assessed in a case-based assignment.

From Courses to Curricula

While all our examples represent semester-long courses, an outcomes map could just as easily be applied to a disciplinary curriculum, program, or major. Developing or revamping a major could proceed the same way as designing a course: working backwards from ultimate to foundational student learning objectives. Members of a department could start at the end of a program, defining as specifically as possible what they want their graduates to be able to

Figure 4.10

Outcomes Map of MGT 390: Introduction to Operations Management,
T. Jefferson Shockley, 2006

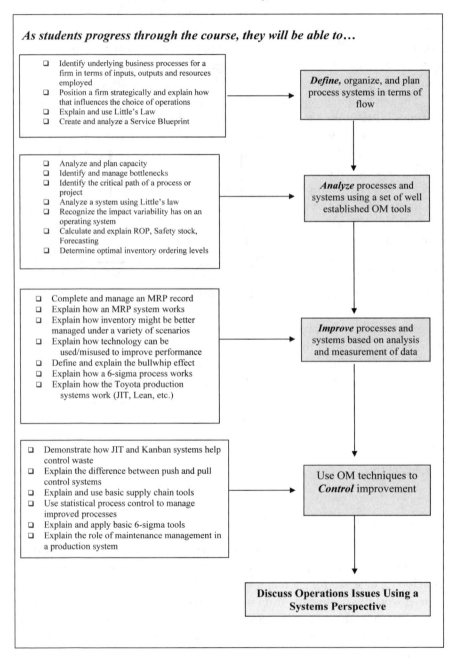

Figure 4.11

Outcomes Map of MGT 318: Management Information Systems,
Pamela S. Galluch, 2007

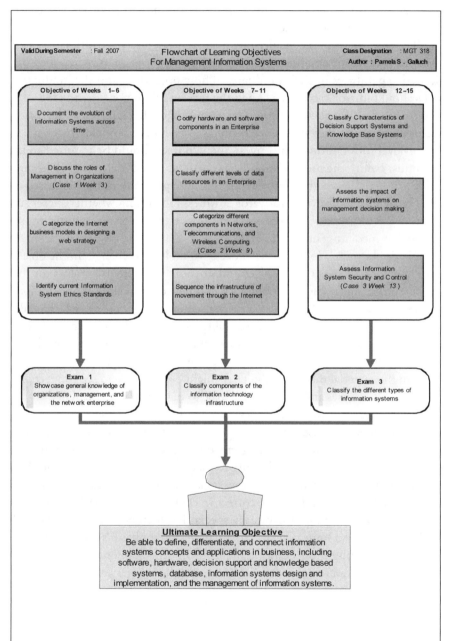

do. Then they could work backwards through the process by which a student could acquire those competencies in a series of courses. Along the way, they would be sharing the student learning objectives they had developed for their own courses, especially their ultimate and their foundational objectives, to see where different courses linked.

The first question the faculty might ask is how closely the ultimate objectives of the capstone and the most advanced, senior-level courses described the desired capabilities of their graduates. These objectives and the graduates' skills should mirror each other. Then the faculty might consider the foundational objectives for these advanced courses. What other courses in the major include objectives that *most directly* prepare students to quickly meet those senior-level foundational objectives? Such courses should be required to be taken just before the most advanced ones. Are any essential sets of skills and abilities not addressed at the optimal times in the program, or not addressed at all? The faculty might work forwards at times, too, asking whether success in meeting the ultimate objectives of course A is essential for meeting the foundational or mediating objectives of course B.

No doubt such a collaborative process would lead to changes in the objectives and content of certain courses and possibly in the requirements for the major. Some courses might be combined and new courses created. In addition, the program would probably have a stricter sequencing of courses, which could make course-staffing needs more predictable. But the real benefit would be students who are better prepared as they move through the courses. They would require less review at the beginning of each course, and they might be able to move through the material more quickly. They might even be able to see connections between their courses and a discernable logic to mastering the discipline.

Many students come into classes with disciplinary amnesia, as if their previous semesters of courses in the major and its prerequisites never happened. Yes, they may vaguely recall learning calculus in their freshman year or in high school, but it was of no immediate use to them back then. So why should they remember it two, three, or even four years later? Sometimes the problem isn't amnesia. Sometimes students are correct in claiming they never had requisite material in past courses. Disciplinary specialties, textbooks, instructors, and students change, so some course content and skill emphases are bound to disappear. A curriculum restructuring might be in order. An outcomes map can serve as a visual tool to conceptualize and move the process along.

5

How Graphics Benefit Course Organization

Over the years I have had many opportunities to observe instructors' reactions to graphically representing the structure of their courses: numerous graphic syllabus workshops, many more course design workshops during which participants constructed an outcomes map, five offerings of my graduate-level College Teaching course, and many private consultations. Instructors have often identified problems with some aspect of their course organization.

In charting an outcomes map, they have pinpointed gaps and transpositions in their initial sequencing of student learning objectives. In a couple of cases, they had their students conducting literature reviews without inserting units on conducting a library search and on analyzing models of published literature reviews. For another example, a few instructors asked their students to perform evaluative tasks on complex course material without first having them paraphrase their understanding of the material and unpack its meaning. What helped these instructors identify holes in the learning process was asking themselves with each objective, "What do my students have to be able to do before they can tackle and succeed in meeting that objective? How likely is it that they have mastered the prerequisite tasks in previous courses?" Indeed, to design a course properly, an instructor should be familiar with the general education and departmental curricula, as well as how some of their colleagues structure their courses.

It is fairly obvious how an outcomes map can reveal gaps and sequencing errors in the design of a learning process. Understanding how a graphic syllabus can help create a cohesive organization of course topics is less obvious.

Using a Graphic Syllabus to Tighten Course Organization

The faculty and graduate students with whom I've worked have commonly reported that designing a graphic syllabus enabled them to identify unnecessary and "tacked-on" topics that didn't fit into the flow of the subject matter. Such topics wound up in the original course layout because the instructor enjoyed teaching them, conducted research on them, used textbooks that included them, or had them in the courses he or she took in college. When instructors considered their motivation, they were willing to delete the outlying topics and free up their course schedule, leaving a little more in-class and homework time for deeper processing and learning-reinforcement activities.

Another problem some instructors diagnosed was a lack of organization in their sequencing of topics, which was most often a product of the textbook's ordering of topics. When they sketched out a graphic syllabus, they were able to see that their chronology of topics failed to mirror the substantive and logical relationships among the topics. They were then able to resequence the topics in some meaningful way. Some of the instructors followed one of the expository structures explained and illustrated in Chapter 3: debate/competition, parallelism, process, sequence/chronology, and categorical hierarchy.

Using a Graphic Syllabus to Organize a Course

Let's use an example to show how starting with a graphic syllabus can produce a more tightly organized course. The Sociology of Religion is a good choice for two reasons. First, a well-educated nonsociologist can understand the terms used to describe typical course topics, and second, the individual instructor has a great deal of discretion in selecting course topics.

Not all subjects allow such discretion. As noted in Chapter 4, the more cumulative, problem-solving disciplines such as mathematics, physics, and engineering have a specified sequencing of the skills students must master in each course. These skills tend to mirror course topics, as every topic involves a problem-solving skill. Not surprisingly, the textbooks in these disciplines do not substantially vary the order of topics. While instructors may not want to significantly change the established order, this does not mean a graphic syllabus is not needed. Coming into the course, students do not understand the logic of the order, and the textbook does not provide the reasoning.

A Sociology of Religion course can address any number of topics. Figure 5.1 lists a representative range of topics as identified in a random selection of 10 Sociology of Religion text syllabi accessible on the web. Note that these are *topics* and not necessarily the words that the syllabi used to identify the subject matter. The tally is an impressive 56 topics, plus 11 specific religions. Almost all of the topics commanded at least one week's worth of attention in the course or courses in which they were found. While all the topics are appropriate for a Sociology of Religion course, some lean toward the political and others toward the economic; some are very U.S.-focused and others, international; several represent an anthropological, historical, or psychological perspective. The point is that not all the topics are related to each other. An instructor can't just pick any 15 or 16 topics of interest and construct a logical, cohesive course out of them. The topics must be chosen so that they interconnect and "flow" together, creating a structure in which students can organize and store the course material.

Figure 5.1
Representative Range of Topics in Sociology of Religion Courses

The Sociological Study of Religion (introduction/overview)
Theoretical and Conceptual Approaches in the Sociology of Religion
How Sociologists Study Religion/Research Methodologies
History of Religion in the United States
Current Status of Religion in the United States
What Freedom of Religion Means (establishment and free exercise clauses)
Civil Religion
Secularization/Secularization Debate
Religion and Rational Choice
Religious Meaning Systems
Religious Experience
Variations of Religious Experience
Variability in Religious Strength
Religion as a Spiritual Quest
Religious Meaning and Institutionalization
Religious Authority and Institutionalization
Religious Belief and Ritual
Modern Religious Conversion
Religious Fundamentalism
Religious Diversity in the United States
Protestant Subcultures in the United States
Religious Patterns in Europe
Religious Organizations (denominations, sects, cults)
Religious Interest Groups
Religious Social Movements (and Countermovements)
Religion and Nationalism

Religion and Colonialism
Religious Conflict and Wars
Religion and Development
Religion and Globalization
Religion and Social Change
Political Economy/Economics of Religion
Religion and the Preservation of Elites
How Religion Affects Decision-Making of Elites
How Religion Affects Political Attitudes and Behavior
How Religion Affects Family and Sexual Behavior
Religious Politics
Religion and the Law
Religion and the Economy
Religion and the Media
Religion and Health Care
Religion and the Internet
Religion and Popular Culture
Religion and Prejudice
Religion and Women
Religion and Youth
Religion and Gender, Sexuality
Religion and Race/Ethnicity
Religion and Education
Religion and Socioeconomic Status (SES)/Class
Protestant Reformation
Religion and the Rise of Capitalism
Religion and Modernity
Future of Religion in Modern Society
Religions Through History
Religions Around the World
Specific Religions
- Islam
- Christianity
- Protestantism
- Catholicism
- Hinduism
- Buddhism
- Taoism
- Confucianism
- Shinto
- Judaism
- Native American

Examples of Well-Structured Courses

The next several figures are graphic syllabi of fictitious but perfectly realistic versions of a Sociology of Religion course. Each graphic displays a different way that a semester's worth of topics could be selected and arranged to create a logical, cohesive course. None of these figures substantially reflects any of the 10 web-accessible text syllabi that provided the 67 possible topics.

Figure 5.2 is a graphic syllabus of a Sociology of Religion course that couches religion within the predominant social-demographic fabric of the United States, with some background on how history wove that fabric. As is typical of such courses, it first introduces students to how sociology treats the subject matter, including the standard theoretical approaches and accompanying research methodologies. The course then turns toward the history of religion and its impact on the institution's current status, with an emphasis on its diversity, both in people's belief systems and in the strength of their faith in these systems. Denominational diversity is explained sociologically in terms of the relationship between people's race and ethnicity, education, and socioeconomic status and their religious affiliation. Variability in strength is anchored by two extremes: religious fundamentalism, which reflects certain Protestant subcultures, and secularization, a topic that includes a debate about how secular Americans actually are. The course closes by speculating on how these two extremes may influence the future of religion in the United States.

Figure 5.3 displays a course organization that starts out the same way as the previous example, then goes in a distinctly more political direction. The main point the course derives from U.S. history is the long-standing tradition of a civil religion. In addition, it integrates religious diversity and its demographic correlates as sources of political differences that give rise to competing interest groups. Such shifting cleavages and coalitions generate a public arena of religion-based politics, one colored with the heritage of a civil religion, which in turn affects how heavily elites weight various religious viewpoints in their decision-making. Through this process, the course concludes, religion becomes another institution in the political economy of modern society.

The next graphic syllabus, displayed in Figure 5.4, shows a Sociology of Religion course that concentrates on the cultural impact of religion in the United States. Once the course introduces students to the types of religious organizations, it addresses the effects of religion on several individual variables and institutions: political attitudes and behavior, including prejudice; family and sexual behavior, including gender-related sexual orientation, and youth; the law—in particular, how it interprets the First Amendment's freedom of religion provisions; popular culture, with a focus on the mass media and the Internet; health care (e.g., faith-based initiatives); and the economy.

Figure 5.2

Graphic Syllabus of a Sociology of Religion Course
with a Social-Demographic Focus on the United States
and Basic Historical Background

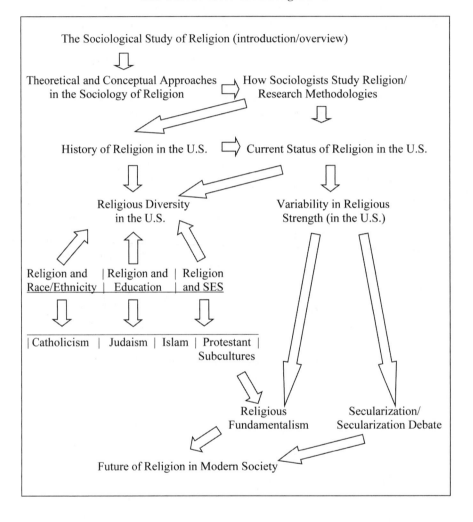

Figure 5.3

Graphic Syllabus of a Sociology of Religion Course
with a Political-Demographic Focus on the United States
and Basic Historical Background

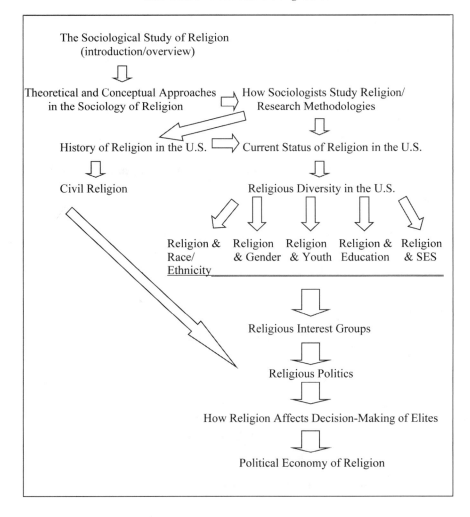

Figure 5.4

Graphic Syllabus of a Sociology of Religion Course
with a Cultural Focus on the Contemporary United States

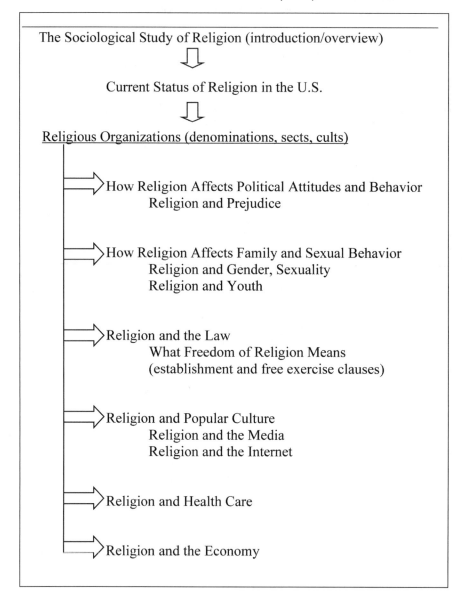

The fourth example, presented in Figure 5.5, takes a broad world-historical perspective on religion. The course first considers the major religions through history and how their histories demonstrate two alternating effects of religion on society: at certain times, deep social change, as when strong social movements generate new ideologies, often spawning conflict and war; and at other times, prolonged social stability, as when religion serves to legitimize the political elites and justifies war to preserve their hegemony. The Protestant Reformation receives in-depth study as an excellent illustration of profound social change that disrupted centuries of Vatican-dominated stability. Then the course examines Max Weber's (1930) thesis that the spread of the Protestant work ethic in certain Western countries fostered the rapid development of capitalism in these locations. The next set of topics traces the impact of religion, first on the capitalist political economy, then on colonialism, and then on the nationalistic movements that challenged colonialism. The course moves on through global history to address the effects of religion on economic development, modernity, and globalization, concluding with predictions on the future of religion in modern society.

The final graphic syllabus, shown in Figure 5.6, displays a Sociology of Religion course with yet another distinctive slant—a predominantly psychological and anthropological perspective. After the standard introduction to the specialty, its theoretical approaches, and its research methodologies, the course examines religion as a spiritual quest, then as a personal experience that has taken many forms. Both of these phenomena give rise to meaning systems, which in turn generate social movements and countermovements, which spread meaning systems across populations. Successful movements eventually become institutionalized, fostering formal dogma and ritual, followed by emergence of religious authorities, such as shamans, priests, and ministers. These authorities formalize and legitimize their power in various types of religious organizations, which eventually enter the political arena as interest groups. But how politically active and influential they become depends on the strength of faith they demand. Compared to denominations, sects and cults tend to demand more, and their belief systems lean more toward the fundamentalist. Given their extremism, they are typically isolated and small, so they rarely participate in large-scale political forums.

Despite the considerable differences among these Sociology of Religion courses, all of them would be quite respectable. The 10 web-accessible text syllabi were just as different from each other. However, the five courses graphically displayed here all have a definite topical "flow" and structure to them. Some might say that each one tells a story about the role of religion in society. In contrast, few of the 10 text syllabi showed such internal cohesion, although

Figure 5.5

Graphic Syllabus of a Sociology of Religion Course
with a World-Historical Focus

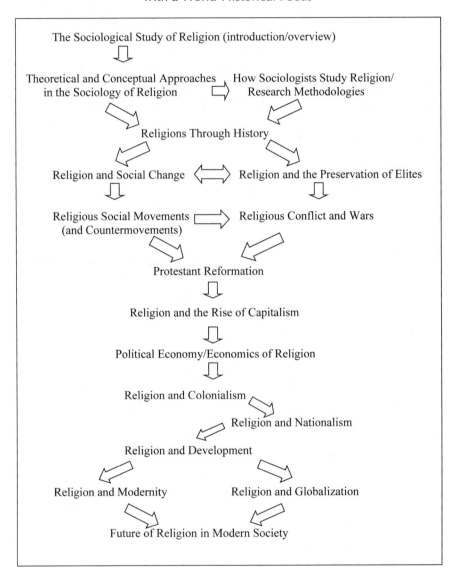

Figure 5.6

Graphic Syllabus of a Sociology of Religion Course
with a Psychological and Anthropological Focus

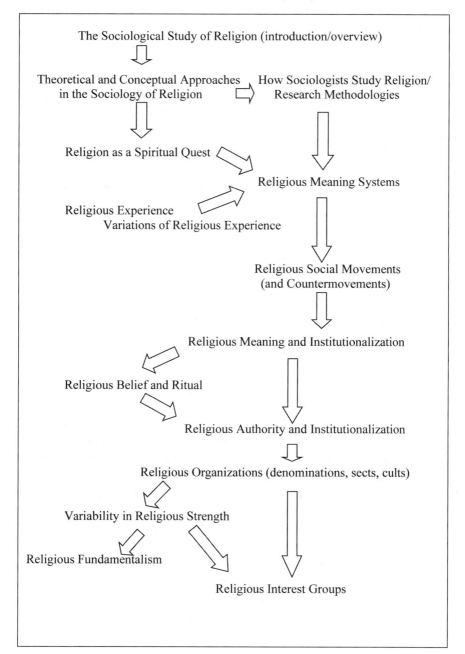

the simple list of topics did not make the gap particularly evident. If nothing else, a graphic syllabus reveals disconnects among topics and helps ensure that the final product is tightly and coherently organized.

You may recall from Chapter 1 that the main reason for organizing a course into a cohesive structure is to help students learn. The human mind can deep-process and retain knowledge only when it can arrange the knowledge in a logically organized, interconnected structure. People with considerable prior knowledge on a given subject only need integrate new knowledge into their existing structure, but those who are new to a subject or whose existing structure is faulty, like so many of our students, need to receive their new knowledge already structured (Anderson, 1984; Bransford, Brown, & Cocking, 1999; Rhem, 1995; Svinicki, 2004). And as the research literature on cognition and learning revealed in Chapter 2, graphics are more effective than words in conveying a structure that the mind can use to assimilate and store new knowledge.

Beyond Student Learning

What lies beyond student learning is what nurtures you as the instructor. Teaching is a giving occupation that sometimes demands more giving than it returns. Adding graphic syllabi and outcomes maps to your course materials may sound like just more tasks to add to your lengthy teaching to-do list. But unlike most items on that list, which benefit your students and your institution, these new tasks offer you some selfish and self-replenishing pleasures.

As I mentioned at the end of Chapter 2, I have watched participants in my graphic syllabi workshops liberate themselves from convention and explore expressive new venues. Some of the most reserved individuals released a flood of metaphorical creativity and artistic flair that surprised even them. You have already seen some of their products in Chapter 3, and you'll see several more in Appendix A.

In longer versions of the workshop, participants designed a "practice" graphic syllabus before attempting their own. They practiced on a fictitious introductory paralegal course, a subject area chosen because none of the participants knew much about it. (They were also free to do this exercise if they chose not to design a graphic syllabus for a course of their own during the workshop.) They were provided only with a list of major topics taken from a real introductory paralegal course (see Figure 5.7), along with paper and/or transparencies and their choice of colored pens. Working with two or three colleagues, they developed markedly different topical organizations and graphic syllabi, all of which followed a logic and flow that they could explain in their presentations. Many of the teams used legal icons and metaphors in their designs (e.g., scales of justice, courthouse facades, gavels). A few situated their course in the metaphor of a trip or adventure through the paralegal field.

Figure 5.7

Topics Given Participants for Organizing a
Fictitious Introductory Paralegal Course in the
Graphic Syllabus Workshop (Long Version)

Legal Research

Regulation of Paralegals

Legal Writing

Employment as a Paralegal

Formal Advocacy Before Administrative Agencies

Legal Interviewing

Legal Analysis

Informal Advocacy Before Administrative Agencies

The American Legal System

Law Office Administration

Legal Investigation

How to Study Law

Whether the participants were designing the fictitious course or one of their own, they all became deeply engrossed in the task and showed genuine originality in recasting abstract, verbal concepts and relationships in visual-spatial arrangements. In the end, they had fun—the kind of fun that accrues from a creative activity that blends the mental with the emotional, freedom with structure, and play with work.

This is the type of activity that injects new life into college teaching. It is energizing, liberating, and revitalizing. It gives the right brain a refreshing new role in an otherwise left-brain endeavor. It gives you, the instructor, a novel way to personalize your teaching and an opportunity to add a creative dimension to your classroom persona.

Appendix A

More Model Graphic Syllabi for Inspiration

Chapter 3 displayed 15 graphic syllabi, four of which were graphic metaphors. They were chosen to illustrate some basic principles. Most of them exemplified designs that reflected five common course structures: debate/competition, parallelism, process, sequence/chronology, and categorical hierarchy. Two of the graphic metaphors illustrated motifs, the umbrella and the floor plan, that can work for many other courses.

This appendix showcases 27 additional graphic syllabi created by faculty and graduate students for undergraduate and graduate courses in a wide range of disciplines. Their varied, content-rich, and eye-catching graphic syllabi will hopefully inspire you to try your hand at composing one yourself. Bear in mind that none of the designers of the graphic syllabi in this book has an art or graphic arts background. Some of the products may look more artistic than others, but that is beside the point. A graphic syllabus is a learning aid for your students, a representation of the structure of the knowledge in your course, not a work of art. In fact, as you go through these examples, you might find yourself learning something about disciplines unfamiliar to you.

If you are at all uncertain about the difference between a graphic syllabus and an outcomes map, you will be able to contrast some graphic syllabi shown here with the outcomes maps displayed in Chapter 4 for the same courses.

The graphic syllabi in this appendix are grouped by discipline in alphabetical order: accounting; chemistry; education; engineering (various fields); English (business writing); finance; food technology; management; parks, recreation, and tourism management; psychology; and veterinary medicine. Most of them were originally composed using color.

Intermediate Accounting

Mary Ann Prater, a licensed CPA and senior lecturer in accounting at Clemson University, designed the graphic syllabus in Figure A.1 for her Intermediate Accounting course. Logically enough, the icon at the top represents an accounting ledger. The graphic flows from left to right and also from top to bottom in "columns" of related topics. Ms. Prater supplied both the associated dates and assigned chapters in the textbook. The added shadowing that she applied to the boxes gives the graphic a three-dimensional look.

This graphic metaphor is an example of the categorical hierarchy model of course organization. The sizes, shapes, and colors of the boxes, as well as their spatial arrangement, distinguish the major organizing topics (along the top row) from the subsumed topics. For instance, "Current and Long-Term Liabilities Balance Sheet" divides into "Current Liabilities" and "Long-Term Debt." In turn, the former breaks down into operational (definite), estimated, and contingent liabilities, and the latter into bonds, two types of convertible bonds, and long-term receivables. The content detail in this graphic syllabus is sufficient to provide a skeletal framework from which students can determine what to study and review for exams.

Figure A.1
Graphic Syllabus of ACCT 313: Intermediate Accounting,
Mary Ann Prater, 2007

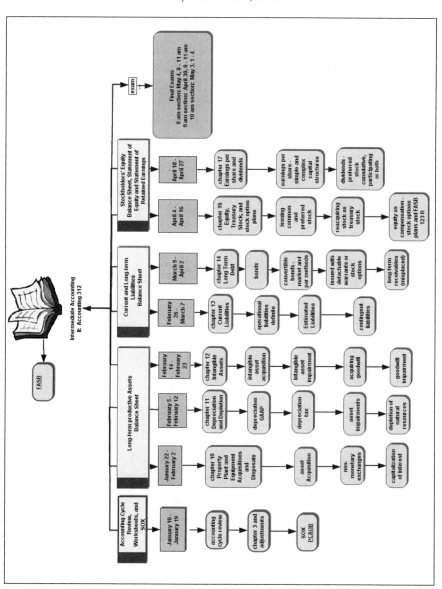

Managerial Accounting Concepts

The pie-shaped graphic syllabus shown in Figure A.2 is, in fact, a collage of brief text and illustrative icons. As it actually resembles a pie, it is best called a graphic metaphor. Miranda Walker, a licensed CPA, assembled it for her Managerial Accounting Concepts course while she was a lecturer in accounting at Clemson University. In personal correspondence (September 11, 2006), she explained her intention to capture the "wholeness" of her field and her conceptual organization of it as 11 "slices" or major topics—specifically, answers to 11 questions essential in business that the different "pieces" of accounting answer. Her major topics are phrased as those questions. The "circle" starts at the top with "What goes into your product's cost?" and proceeds around to pose additional questions about business costs, the products made and sold, special decisions, the budget, and major investments. The key issue in each question is represented in one or more appropriate cutout images.

Figure A.2
Graphic Syllabus of ACCT 202: Managerial Accounting Concepts,
Miranda Walker, 2006

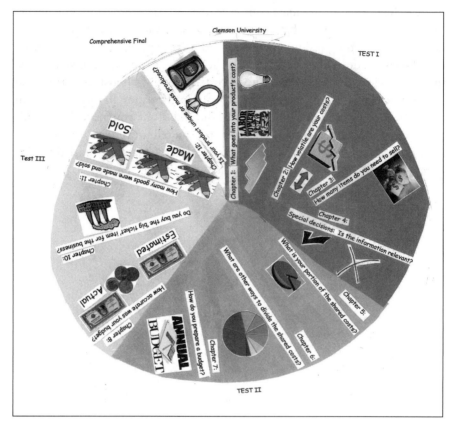

Chemistry: Statistical Thermodynamics

Perhaps the simplest graphic syllabus in this book's collection belongs to Dr. Stephen J. Stuart, associate professor of chemistry at Clemson University. Figure A.3 shows that his graduate course, Statistical Thermodynamics, generally follows the organization of the textbook he used. Most of the topics are ordered in a linear progression down the middle of the page, but three topics are set off to one side or the other. One of these, Classical Statistical Mechanics, involves review, but it also enhances students' comprehension of the ideal Polyatomic Gas and, a few weeks later, Quantum Statistics. In turn, Quantum Statistics informs the topic of Crystals at the end of the course. Boltz/FD/BE Statistics are also review topics, but they are essential to students' understanding of the ideal Monatomic Gas and, weeks later, Quantum Statistics. The number of lectures allocated to each topic is listed to the far left.

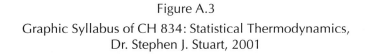

Figure A.3

Graphic Syllabus of CH 834: Statistical Thermodynamics, Dr. Stephen J. Stuart, 2001

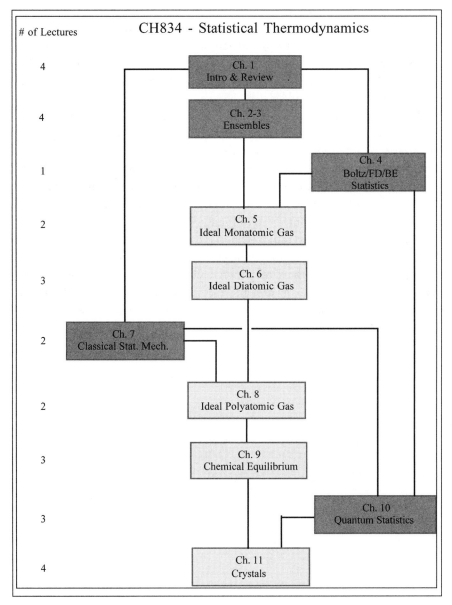

Methods of Teaching Language Arts and History–Social Science

In Figure 3.4 in Chapter 3, we examined a graphic syllabus designed by Dr. Cynthia Desrochers, a professor of education and founding director of the Center for Excellence in Teaching and Learning at California State University–Northridge. It displays the organization of her course, Methods of Teaching Language Arts and History-Social Science, structured around the parallels between the school curriculum (its student learning objectives) and the strategies used for instruction and assessment.

Figure A.4 shows a completely different graphic syllabus for the same course, which was designed one semester later. Dr. Desrochers challenged her class to try creating the graphic and based her redesigned version on what one of her students produced. Moving in several directions rather than only downward, this revision contains much the same information as the first—the same major topics and subtopics, the same classes/weeks in the semester, and the same assignments due—but the layout and design features are very different. The major topics are boxed rather than in larger type. These topics, along with their subtopics, are circled, and these circles are interrelated. The "General Strategies" for instruction have their own circle that provides a background for those specific to the language arts and history-social sciences. Furthermore, the curving arrow indicates the utility of the language arts to the study of history and the social sciences.

Figure A.4
Graphic Syllabus of EED 570M:
Methods of Teaching Language Arts and History-Social Science,
Dr. Cynthia Desrochers, 2001

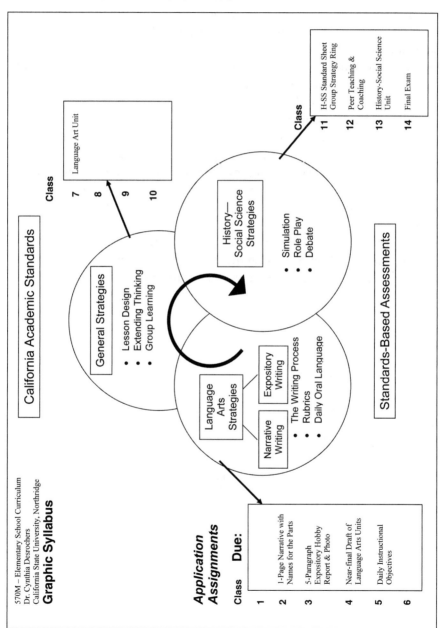

College Teaching

You may recall from Chapter 4 the outcomes map I developed for my graduate-level course at Clemson University, VT ED 876: College Teaching (Figure 4.9). The course design aimed to interrelate Fink's (2003) categories of learning to create significant learning experiences.

With the focus on content topics, the graphic syllabus for this course looks quite different (see Figure A.5). As it moves only from top to bottom, it has a very simple design. The course has three main parts that are not evident in the outcomes map: the first about today's students, the second on designing and developing a course, and the third on starting a college-level teaching career.

Within the second part, which takes most of the semester, are three subparts. The first subpart is on overall course design around student learning objective/outcomes (including text and graphic syllabus development). The next is on an array of effective learning/teaching methods (e.g., teaching students how to read academic material, writing-to-learn activities, sound uses of technology, cooperative learning, experiential learning). The last subpart is on multiple forms of assessment (student, institutional, and teaching).

The third and final part of the course is organized around the career-launching process, from preparing the necessary documents for the job market, to finding job announcements, to obtaining and keeping a faculty position.

Figure A.5
Graphic Syllabus of VTED 876: College Teaching,
Dr. Linda B. Nilson, 2006

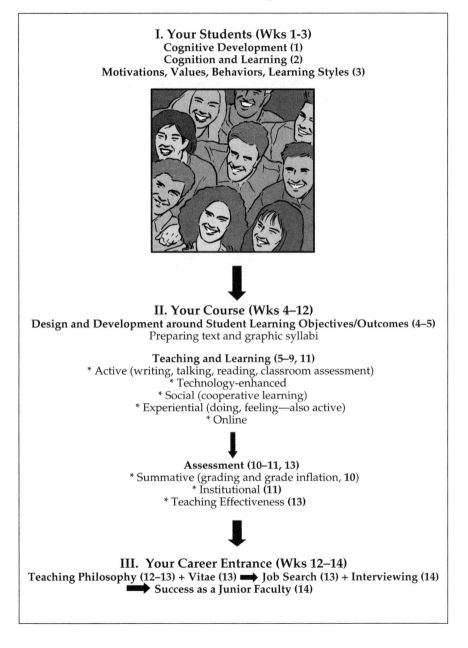

I. Your Students (Wks 1-3)
Cognitive Development (1)
Cognition and Learning (2)
Motivations, Values, Behaviors, Learning Styles (3)

II. Your Course (Wks 4–12)
Design and Development around Student Learning Objectives/Outcomes (4–5)
Preparing text and graphic syllabi

Teaching and Learning (5–9, 11)
* Active (writing, talking, reading, classroom assessment)
* Technology-enhanced
* Social (cooperative learning)
* Experiential (doing, feeling—also active)
* Online

Assessment (10–11, 13)
* Summative (grading and grade inflation, **10**)
* Institutional **(11)**
* Teaching Effectiveness **(13)**

III. Your Career Entrance (Wks 12–14)
Teaching Philosophy (12–13) + Vitae (13) ➡ Job Search (13) + Interviewing (14)
➡ **Success as a Junior Faculty (14)**

Design and Implementation of Programming Languages

Unlike any other graphic syllabus in this book's collection, the one in Figure A.6 moves from both the top and the bottom to the middle. As its creator, Clemson University computer science professor Dennis E. ("Steve") Stevenson, explained, his students actually build the products named in the long rectangle in the middle of the graphic—first, the scanner, then the parser, and so on. But to figure out how to build these things, students must first have a working command of the topics above and below (D. E. Stevenson, personal correspondence, September 16, 2006).

The course, Design and Implementation of Programming Languages, addresses the topics shown above the rectangle in the first three weeks of the course. All of these topics pertain to semniotics, which is about how languages work. In fact, Dr. Stevenson's graphic syllabus features concept maps of the interrelationships among the key ideas in semniotics, and his course follows that map. Below the rectangle are pure computer science topics that the course covers during later weeks in the semester. Unlike the more abstract subject of language, this material is technical—specifically, computing theory and its derivatives and project management in software engineering. By the end of the course, students are integrating semniotics and computer engineering to construct real products (D. E. Stevenson, personal correspondence, September 16, 2006).

Figure A.6
Graphic Syllabus of CPSC 428/628:
Design and Implementation of Programming Languages,
Dr. Dennis E. ("Steve") Stevenson, 2006

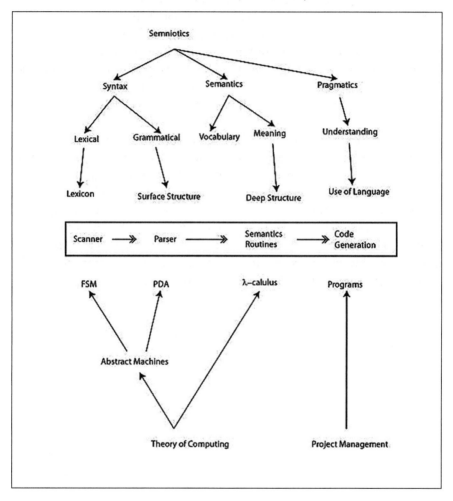

Environmental Risk Assessment

It is well worth displaying both the topic schedule from the text syllabus and the graphic syllabus of Environmental Risk Assessment, a graduate course in environmental engineering and sciences taught by Dr. Robert A. Fjeld, a named professor in Clemson University's School of the Environment. The text version in Figure A.7 separates the major topics from the subtopics, yet the relationships among the major topics and even among certain major topics and their subtopics are not all clear. The lengthy list gives the impression that the field is just a string of unrelated topics, perhaps with one exception: One might correctly surmise that all the terms ending with *transport* share the same category.

Contrast the text version with the graphic syllabus in Figure A.8. Here it is clear that the thrust of the course is the risk calculation process. The graphic indicates that this process involves four types of analyses in a given order (release, environmental transport, exposure, and consequence). The Laplace transform technique is used in the first two types of analysis, modeling in the second type, and variability and uncertainty analysis in the fourth type. The graphic syllabus also suggests that the risk calculation process makes risk management possible and moves environmental risk assessment from the purely technical domain into the public and administrative realm.

Figure A.7
Edited Text Syllabus of EE&S 880: Environmental Risk Assessment, Dr. Robert A. Fjeld, 2006

EE&S 880 - ENVIRONMENTAL RISK ASSESSMENT
SPRING 2006, Professor Robert A. Fjeld

An assessment of the human health risk of contaminants released to the environment. Quantitative risk assessment is developed and applied to various environmental pathways and classes of contaminants.

TEXTS: *Environmental Risk Analysis (Draft)*, R. A. Fjeld, N. A. Eisenburg, & K. Compton, 2006.
Risk Assessment Methods, V. T. Covello & M. W. Merkhofer, Plenum Press, New York, 1993.

	MAJOR TOPIC	SUB-TOPICS	CHAPTER ASSIGNMENT	PROBLEM SET ASSIGNMENT
1/12	COURSE INTRODUCTION	Course Administration Overview of Environmental Risk Assessment	1	#1 Out
1/17	RELEASE ANALYSIS	Risk Assessment Modeling Laplace Transform Technique Contaminants, Emission Rate	2.1–2.2	
1/19		Emission Control, Accident Analysis	3	
1/24	ENVIRONMENTAL TRANSPORT ANALYSIS - THEORY	Contaminant Transport Equation (CTE)	2	
1/26		Solutions to the CTE	4	#1 In, #2 Out
1/31		Solutions to the CTE	4	
2/2	ENVIRONMENTAL TRANSPORT ANALYSIS - APPLICATIONS	Atmospheric Transport	7	#2 In, #3 Out
2/7		Atmospheric Transport	7	
2/9		Atmospheric Transport	7	#3 In, #4 Out
2/14		Surface Water Transport	5	
2/16		Surface Water Transport	5	#4 In, #5 Out
2/21		Ground Water Transport	6	
2/23		Ground Water Transport	6	#5 In, #6 Out
2/28		Food Chain Transport	8	
3/2	EXPOSURE ANALYSIS		9	#6 In
3/7	CONSEQUENCE ANALYSIS	Introduction Toxicity Fundamentals	10	
3/9		**Hourly Exam #1**		#7 Out
3/14		Toxicity Fundamentals:	10	
3/16		Toxicity Fundamentals Mechanisms of Cancer Induction	10	#7 In
3/28		Dose-Response	10	Term Project Out
3/30		Dose-Response	10	PS 8 Out
4/4		Risk Characterization Parameters	10	
4/6	MODELING VARIABILITY AND UNCERTAINTY ANALYSIS	Model Development Variability and Risk Characterization		PS 8 In
4/11		Risk Curves Distribution Functions		PS 8 In
4/13		Variability Analysis Monte Carlo Method		
4/18		Error Propagation Uncertainty Analysis		
4/20	RISK MANAGEMENT	Introduction Public Involvement Regulatory Applications		
4/25		**Hourly Exam #2**		PS 9 Out
4/27		Multi-attribute Decision Analysis, Ecological Risk Assessment Risk Assessment	13	Term Project In

Figure A.8

Graphic Syllabus of EE&S 880: Environmental Risk Assessment,
Dr. Robert A. Fjeld, 2006

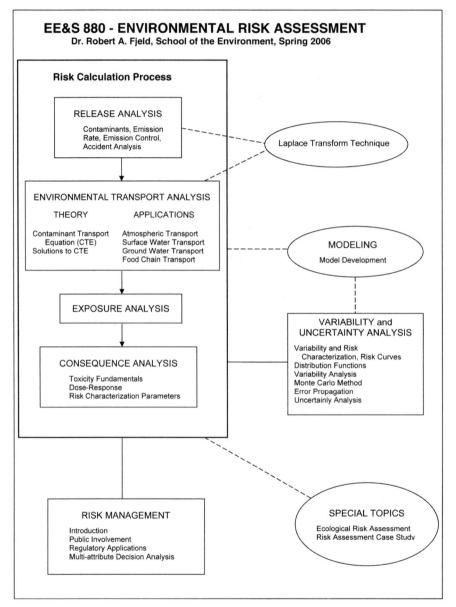

Systems Programming Concepts for Computer Engineering

Dr. Melissa C. Smith is an assistant professor in the Holcombe Department of Electrical and Computer Engineering at Clemson University and designer of the only two-page graphic syllabus in this collection. As shown in Figure A.9, her graphic meanders from side to side and progresses down a pathway of topics, some of which have complex interrelationships (see the second quarter of the course).

Dr. Smith's creation has some unusual features that are worth highlighting. It uses several icons in typical ways—a head and book for review, question marks for tests, and code graphics—but it also uses two icons metaphorically: a physical building for the task of program building and a book-type library image for the computer-science type (a collection of routines stored in a file). Perhaps the most distinctive features of this graphic syllabus are its enclosures, many of which visually symbolize the topics so well that they approximate icons—for example, those around "Memory Map," "Arrays/Strings," "Structures," "Pointers," "File I/O Buffering File Systems," and "Streams/Devices." One final noteworthy aspect of this graphic is its inclusion of the lab topics and their links to the topics of the main class meetings. It is important that students can see the connections between labs and the rest of the course.

Figure A.9 (page 1)

Graphic Syllabus of ECE 222:
Systems Programming Concepts for Computer Engineering,
Dr. Melissa C. Smith, 2006

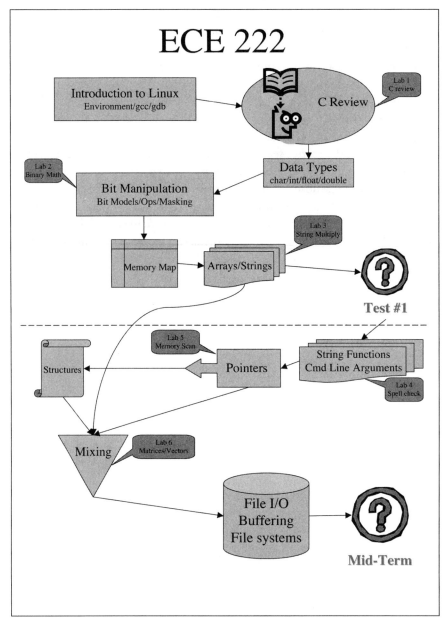

Figure A.9 (page 2)

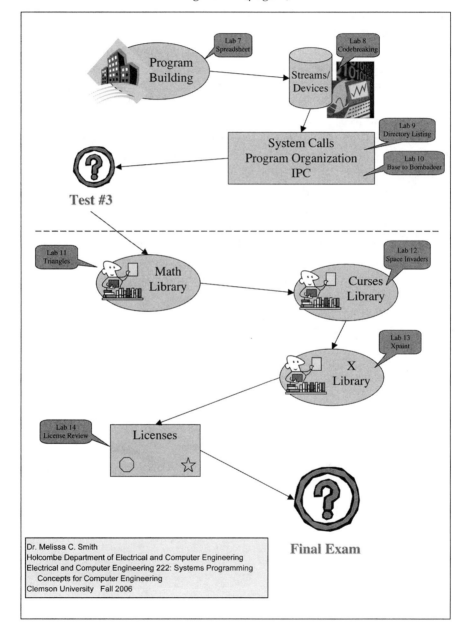

English: Business Writing

A lecturer in English at Clemson University, Mr. Philip Randall used his Business Writing graphic syllabus (see Figure A.10) to "walk students through the goals and purposes of the course on the first day of class" and found it to be "a great teaching tool" (personal correspondence, August 28, 2006). His graphic has a look and feel all its own—not of a flowchart but of a structure, and intentionally so. Mr. Randall's emphasis in this course was on foundational skills and principles that he wanted his students to practice in different business communication assignments throughout the semester. He called the main skills "action grammar" and the primary principles "SIDAP" (Simple, Informal, Direct, Active, Personal) and "the 14 points" from the textbook for the course, Joanne Feierman's *Action Grammar: Fast, No-Hassle Answers on Everyday Usage and Punctuation.* Dr. Randall also assigned student teams various readings that explain or illustrate these skills and principles.

This graphic syllabus does not lack flow through time. Note the weeks of the semester subtly arrayed along the bottom. Superimposed on this "calendar" are the two major parts of the course—the first, on how to get a job, then on how to keep one—as well as the different types of communication (including résumés, cover letters, company research, and interviewing), each of which receives about two weeks of attention. Set in columns, these types of communication appear to support the crowning principle, "Confidence is based on competence." Again, this was Mr. Randall's intention.

Figure A.10
Graphic Syllabus of ENG 304: Business Writing,
Mr. Philip Randall, 2006

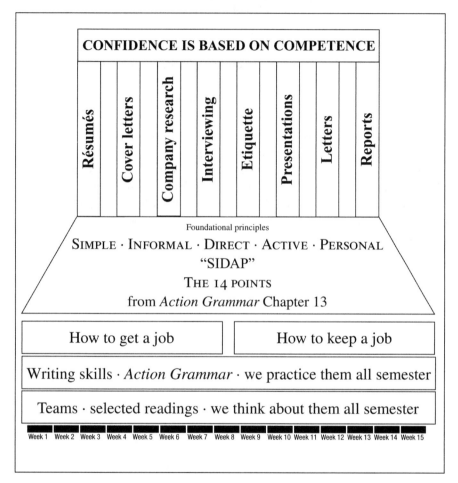

Introductory Finance

The designer of the graphic syllabus shown in Figure A.11 is Dr. Ernest N. Biktimirov, an associate professor in the Faculty of Business at Brock University in St. Catherine's, Ontario, Canada. He is no stranger to using visuals in teaching. In fact, he and I have published three articles on the topic (Biktimirov & Nilson, 2003, 2006, 2007). Dr. Biktimirov had already made extensive use of mind maps when he composed this graphic syllabus for his introductory finance course.

Dr. Biktimirov's graphic moves from top to bottom overall, but also from left to right through the middle of the semester. It displays both the major topics and their respective subtopics in interlinked "blocks." Given the amount of content detail in each block, this graphic syllabus can serve as a student's skeletal framework for study and review, as can Ms. Prater's for Intermediate Accounting (Figure A.1). These blocks also identify the relevant textbook chapter(s) and week(s) in the semester. Dr. Biktimirov highlights the midterm and final exams in shaded hexagons that resemble stop signs, suggesting times to pause in the progression of topics.

Figure A.11

Graphic Syllabus of FIN 101: Introductory Finance,
Dr. Ernest N. Biktimirov, 2002

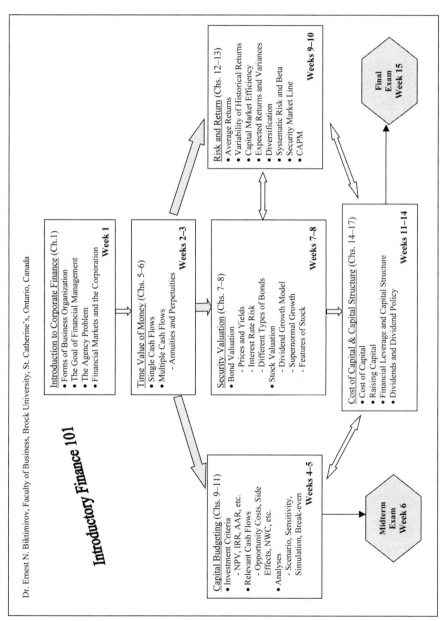

Food Science

You may recall Dr. Aubrey Coffee's graphic syllabus of her food science course, Culinary Techniques, in Chapter 3 (Figure 3.12). She also designed one for The Evolution of Gingerbread, a student-team research project in Clemson University's undergraduate research program, Creative Inquiry (see Figure A.12). Similar to Dr. Smith's (Figure A.9), Dr. Coffee's graphic syllabus meanders its way down the page, laying out a complex strategy for identifying and collecting relevant data on the history of gingerbread. The graphic makes this strategy ever so clear: Students begin by finding recipes and researching their historical and geographic origins. Then they test the recipes and analyze the products on various sensory dimensions (emotion, appearance, aroma, texture, sensation, and basic tastes). Ultimately, students compare, contrast, and come to conclusions about the relative quality of the different gingerbreads. More importantly, they learn how to conduct research on the history and cultural variability of any food the way food scientists do it.

Figure A.12
Graphic Syllabus of FDSC 421: The Evolution of Gingerbread,
Creative Inquiry Undergraduate Research Team,
Dr. Aubrey Coffee, 2006

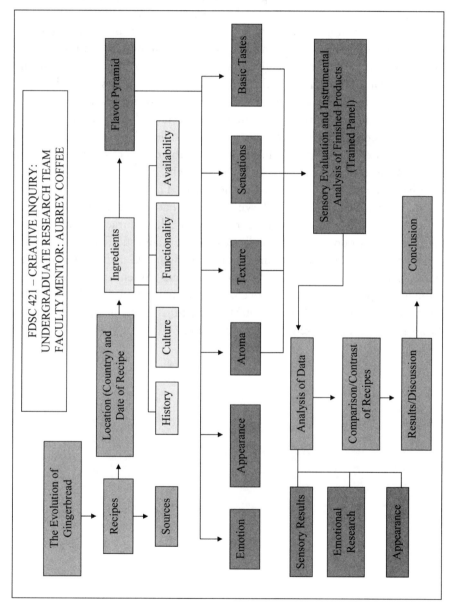

Creativity and Innovation in Business

Kathleen Kegley, a lecturer in management at Clemson University, teaches most of her courses online, including MBA 899: Creativity and Innovation in Business. Figure A.13 shows the graphic syllabus she developed for this graduate course. Perhaps its most unusual feature is its absence of flow through time. This flow is not as necessary in a self-paced online course. The graphic arrays course information coming out from the center, as does a mind map. The scroll in the upper middle gives basic course and instructor information, while the lower middle displays the student learning objectives (e.g., idea generation, creative attitude, risk-taking) and cornerstone descriptors of the course's approach to learning (authentic, experiential, constructivist) in a three-dimensional image that appropriately resembles a base.

The rest of the graphic syllabus lays out the contract grading system, which makes sense since, in Ms. Kegley's system, a student's grade reflects what he or she has actually learned in the course. The images in the upper left corner, the goalposts and football, symbolize the nature of contract grading: A student either meets or doesn't meet the terms of the contract—that is, he or she either does or doesn't get the ball between the goalposts. The other corners display the contractual requirements of an A, B, and C. A higher grade demands that a student successfully complete the assignments required for one grade lower, plus additional, more challenging assignments (K. Kegley, personal correspondence, May 17, 2005). The whimsical icons echo aspects of the assignments and lighten the graphic's mood.

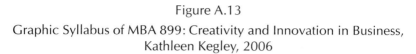

Figure A.13
Graphic Syllabus of MBA 899: Creativity and Innovation in Business,
Kathleen Kegley, 2006

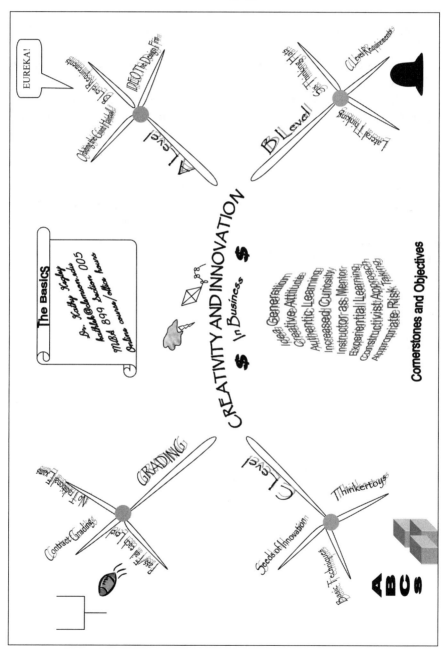

Small Business Management

Dr. Teresa Isabelle Daza Campbell, a management professor at Pima Community College–West Campus, designed the graphic syllabus in Figure A.14 for her Small Business Management course. She organized the material into a flat (one-layer) categorical hierarchy, which may call to mind the graphic syllabus in Chapter 3 (Figure 3.14) developed by Dr. Robert W. Schwartz for CME (Ceramic and Materials Engineering) 302: Phase Equilibria, which he taught at Clemson University several years ago.

Both graphics are similar in that the top center box sets off the introductory material, after which the course proceeds through three major sections. In Dr. Campbell's case, those sections identify the three categories of issues involved in successful small business creation and management (marketing, financial, and operations). The issues themselves (including the introductory ones) are presented as questions that must be answered.

Also included is the semester-long assignment, Writing an Effective Business Plan, which ties together the three sections of material at the end of the course. Given its level of detail, this graphic syllabus can double as a study and review sheet for students.

Figure A.14

Graphic Syllabus of MGT 124: Small Business Management,
Dr. Teresa Isabelle Daza Campbell, 2001

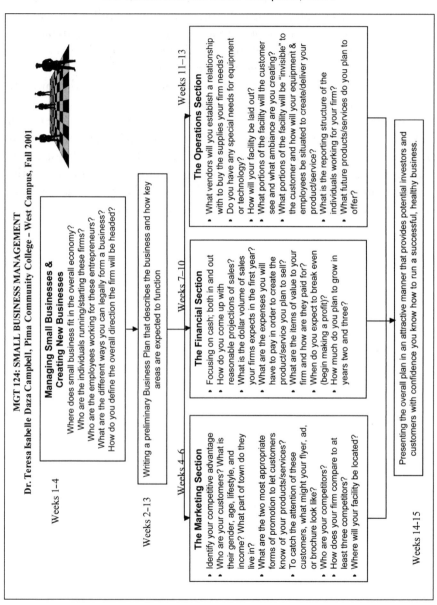

MGT 124: SMALL BUSINESS MANAGEMENT
Dr. Teresa Isabelle Daza Campbell, Pima Community College – West Campus, Fall 2001

Weeks 1–4

**Managing Small Businesses &
Creating New Businesses**

Where does small business fit in the overall economy?
Who are the individuals running/starting these firms?
Who are the employees working for these entrepreneurs?
What are the different ways you can legally form a business?
How do you define the overall direction the firm will be headed?

Weeks 2–13 Writing a preliminary Business Plan that describes the business and how key areas are expected to function

Weeks 4–6

The Marketing Section

- Identify your competitive advantage
- Who are your customers? What is their gender, age, lifestyle, and income? What part of town do they live in?
- What are the two most appropriate forms of promotion to let customers know of your products/services?
- To catch the attention of these customers, what might your flyer, ad, or brochure look like?
- Who are your competitors?
- How does your firm compare to at least three competitors?
- Where will your facility be located?

Weeks 7–10

The Financial Section

- Focusing on cash; both in and out
- How do you come up with reasonable projections of sales?
- What is the dollar volume of sales your firms expects in the first year?
- What are the expenses you will have to pay in order to create the product/service you plan to sell?
- What are the items of value to your firm and how are they paid for?
- When do you expect to break even (begin making a profit)?
- How much do you plan to grow in years two and three?

Weeks 11–13

The Operations Section

- What vendors will you establish a relationship with to buy the supplies your firm needs?
- Do you have any special needs for equipment or technology?
- How will your facility be laid out?
- What portions of the facility will the customer see and what ambiance are you creating?
- What portions of the facility will be "invisible" to the customer and how will your equipment & employees be situated to create/deliver your product/service?
- What is the reporting structure of the individuals working for your firm?
- What future products/services do you plan to offer?

Weeks 14–15

Presenting the overall plan in an attractive manner that provides potential investors and customers with confidence you know how to run a successful, healthy business.

Project Management

A Ph.D. candidate in management at Clemson University, Nicholas Roberts composed a table-like graphic syllabus for his Project Management course (Figure A.15). His graphic is the only one in this book's collection that displays a course organization in table format, and this choice served his purpose. His aim, which a mere listing of topics could not accomplish, was to show project management as a five-stage process—initiating, planning, executing, controlling, and closing—that cuts across nine logistic matters that must be managed in a certain order during the process: integration, scope, time, cost, quality, human resources, communication, risk, and procurement. The overall direction of Mr. Roberts' graphic syllabus is from top to bottom, as the weeks of the semester indicate. But within the time allocated to a given logistic matter, the graphic also moves from left to right across the columns. As the graphic clearly shows, each logistic matter becomes salient in at least one and in as many as all five stages of the project management process.

Figure A.15

Graphic Syllabus of MGT 411: Project Management,
Nicholas Roberts, 2007

MGT 411: Project Management, Fall 2007 –
Graphic Syllabus

Knowledge Area Processes	Initiating	Planning	Executing	Controlling	Closing
Project Integration Management (weeks 1–2)	Develop Project Charter; Develop Project Scope Statement	Develop Project Management Plan	Manage Project Execution	Integrated Change Control; Monitor Project Work	Close Project
Project Scope Management (weeks 3–4)		Scope Planning; Scope Definition; Create WBS		Scope Verification; Scope Control	
Project Time Management (weeks 5–6)		Activity Definition; Activity Sequencing; Activity Resource Estimating; Activity Duration Estimating; Schedule Development		Schedule Control	
Project Cost Management (weeks 7–8)		Cost Estimating; Cost Budgeting		Cost Control	
Project Quality Management (week 9)		Quality Planning	Perform Quality Assurance	Perform Quality Control	
Project Human Resource Management (week 11)		Human Resource Planning	Acquire Project Team; Develop Project Team	Manage Project Team	
Project Communication Management (week 11)		Communications Planning	Information Distribution	Performance Reporting; Manage Stakeholders	
Project Risk Management (week 12–13)		Risk Management Planning; Risk Identification; Qualitative Risk Analysis; Quantitative Risk Analysis; Risk Response Planning		Risk Monitoring & Control	
Project Procurement Management (week 14)		Plan Purchases & Acquisitions; Plan Contracting	Request Seller Responses; Select Sellers	Contract Administration	Contract Closure

Nicholas Roberts, Clemson University

Database Design and Administration

Another Ph.D. candidate in management at Clemson University, J. Christopher Zimmer, created the graphic syllabus in Figure A.16 for a hypothetical Database Design and Administration course he expects to teach in his first academic position. He made the syllabus clean, simple, and easy to follow. Novices who know next to nothing about the subject matter, like many of us, can still understand how he presents and organizes it.

The starting point of Mr. Zimmer's course is relational algebra, and he first leads his students through the theoretical foundation of E-R (Entity-Relationship) diagramming, then into physical applications, then through database design and ultimately database building and administration. Even if the vocabulary is strange, a student can see how the subject matter builds over the weeks.

Mr. Zimmer enhances the utility of his graphic by designating the week in the semester for each topic in the right-hand column. To add interest, he varies the shapes of the enclosures but uses the same shapes for topics on the same level of analysis—for example, "Theoretical Realm" and "Physical Realm," "Build a Database" and "Administer a Database." He also catches the eye with a few appropriate icons at the top, especially the whimsical stick-drawn, happy-faced user.

Portions of this text and Mr. Zimmer's graphic syllabus were published in *Teaching and Learning Creatively: Inspirations and Reflections,* edited by P. A. Connor-Greene, et al. © 2006 by Parlor Press. Used by permission.

Figure A.16

Graphic Syllabus of MGT: Database Design and Administration,
J. Christopher Zimmer, 2004

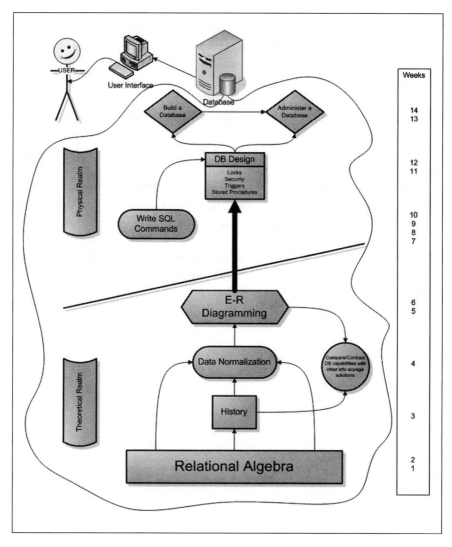

The next seven graphic syllabi were composed by Ph.D. candidates at Clemson University—the first five in management and the last two in parks, recreation, and tourism management. All the accompanying outcomes maps are displayed in Chapter 4 so you can compare and contrast both graphics for the same courses. In a couple of cases, the graphic syllabus bears a resemblance to the map because the designer used the same software and/or a similar layout. But in most cases, the two graphics look completely different.

Decision Models for Management

Uzay Damali's graphic syllabus of Decision Models for Management (see Figure A.17) doesn't look anything like his flowchart-like outcomes map (Figure 4.1) for the same course. In fact, it is a graphic metaphor, as he visually equated progress in his course—from background knowledge to basic application and analysis to advanced application—with climbing a staircase in a business setting. He added depth to his metaphorical image with color and shadowing. Interestingly, his topical organization and his outcomes map break the course into different units—the former into three "stages" of classes (1–2, 3–12, and 13–31) and the latter into three learning sequences of classes (1–9, 10–18, and 19–31). The graphic syllabus flows along a left to right diagonal, which is unique in this collection.

Figure A.17

Graphic Syllabus of MGT 312: Decision Models for Management,
Uzay Damali, 2007

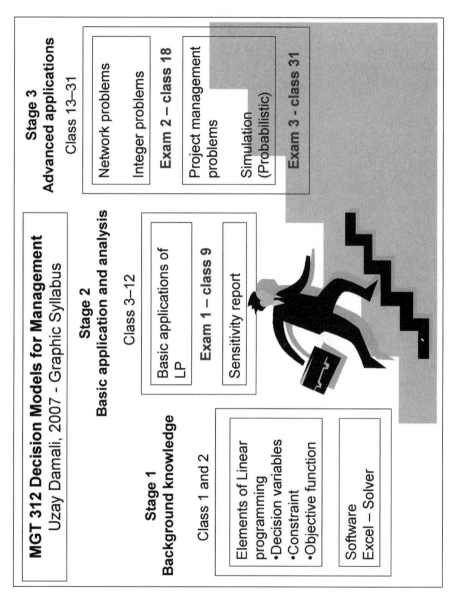

Managerial Decision Modeling

Despite somewhat different course titles, Mohammed Raja's graphic syllabus (see Figure A.18) is for the same course as Mr. Damali's, yet they don't resemble each other in the least. While Mr. Damali divided his course into three sections, Mr. Raja broke it into two major sections, "Deterministic Modeling" and "Probabilistic Modeling," and within the former, distinguished two subsections, "Linear Programming Models" and "Sensitivity and Network Flow Models." Only "Simulation" falls under "Probabilistic Modeling." As the thickest arrows indicate, both "Deterministic Modeling" and "Probabilistic Modeling" inform "Project Management," the former through the critical path method and the latter through the project evaluation review technique. Mr. Raja's graphic includes considerable content detail and interrelationships among topics, something that a list of topics could never capture. In addition, the way he shadowed and colored the smaller enclosures lends a three-dimensional look. While the graphic's design is that of a flowchart that moves predominantly from left to right and from top to bottom, it looks nothing like the flowchart he developed for his outcomes map (Figure 4.3).

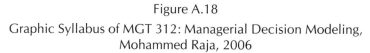

Figure A.18

Graphic Syllabus of MGT 312: Managerial Decision Modeling,
Mohammed Raja, 2006

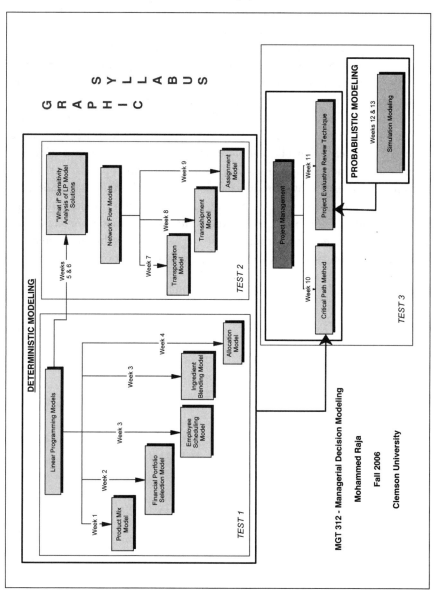

Strategic Management of Information Technology

In this book's collection, no graphic syllabus is more striking and, in its original form, more colorful than Samuel Otim's amazing creation for his course, Strategic Management of Information Technology (see Figure A.19). It is, in fact, a graphic metaphor, as it superimposes the organization of his course on a hot air balloon. Mr. Otim's metaphor makes the statement that IT (information technology)/IS (information systems) trends, the types of IS, IS infrastructure, IS planning, and IS implementation (acquisition, outsourcing, and management) are not only interconnected but also "carry" or support the strategic uses and business value of IT/IS. In addition, the goals of the user organization and those of a specific IT/IS also impact these strategic uses and value. All this means that IT/IS applications vary in their utility and value to a given business, and managers must assess their application options, rather than assuming that every innovation or expansion will benefit their organization.

For the same course, Mr. Otim's outcomes map was a simple, three-stage flowchart (Figure 4.4). But it complements his graphic metaphor in guiding students to competency in assessing the strategic uses and value of different information technologies and systems for different organizations.

Figure A.19

Graphic Syllabus of MGT 490:
Strategic Management of Information Technology,
Samuel Otim, 2007

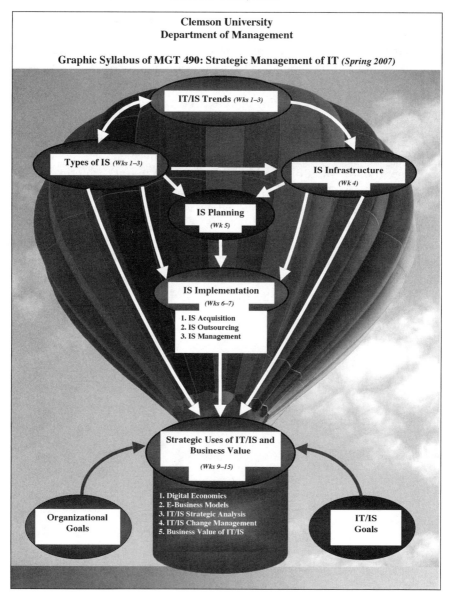

Introduction to Operations Management

The previous three graphic syllabi bore no or little resemblance to their counterpart outcomes maps, but the graphic syllabus in Figure A.20 largely does mirror its outcomes map (Figure 4.10). Both were composed by T. Jefferson Shockley for his Introduction to Operations Management course, and they have some features in common. They both have a flowchart design that moves from left to right, then from top to bottom. The major course topics listed down the middle of the graphic syllabus—"Defining process flow," "Analysis of systems," "Process of improvement," and "Controlling improvement"— match the major student learning objectives going down the right side of the outcomes map—"*Define,* organize, and plan process systems in terms of flow," "*Analyze* processes and systems . . . ," "*Improve* processes and systems . . . ," and "Use OM techniques to *control* improvement."

In general, the subtopics and subobjectives also reflect each other. However, the capstone topic, "OM as a Strategic Advantage," is somewhat distinct from the ultimate learning objective, which is to "Discuss Operations Issues Using a Systems Perspective."

Mr. Shockley also sprinkles a few icons in his graphic syllabus and inserts test information. The parallels between his graphic syllabus and his outcomes map are not at all problematic, which only shows that these two graphics don't *have* to be very different to be effective.

Figure A.20
Graphic Syllabus of MGT 390: Introduction to Operations Management,
T. Jefferson Shockley, 2006

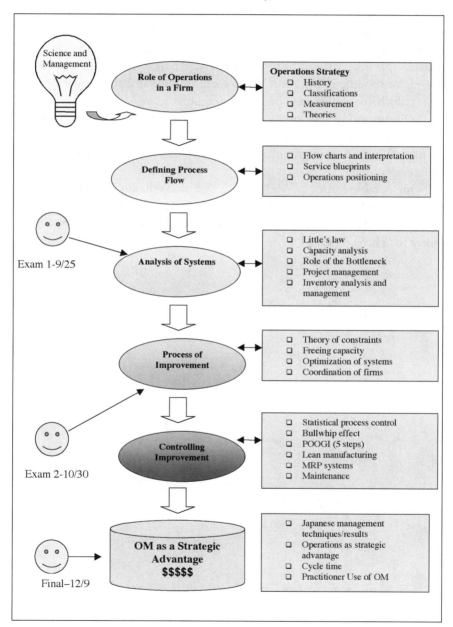

Management Information Systems

Pamela S. Galluch designed a graphic syllabus for her Management Information Systems course that at first glance looks somewhat like a table (see Figure A.21). The weeks are listed down the far left side, the three case studies down the far right side, and the textbook chapter assignments between them. But unlike a typical table, it contains three flowcharts linking related groups of chapters that are separated by exams. Each flowchart displays the organization of a major module in the course, and these are the same three modules that Ms. Galluch's outcomes map highlights (Figure 4.11).

Superimposing the outcomes map on the graphic syllabus reveals that Ms. Galluch has a particular student learning objective for each assigned chapter. While the two graphics appear to be quite different, they complement each other.

One notable feature of Ms. Galluch's graphic syllabus is the creative way she uses arrows coming down from the first two exams to indicate what material the final exam will cover (everything after Exam 1) and will not cover (everything before Exam 1).

Figure A.21
Graphic Syllabus of MGT 318: Management Information Systems,
Pamela S. Galluch, 2006

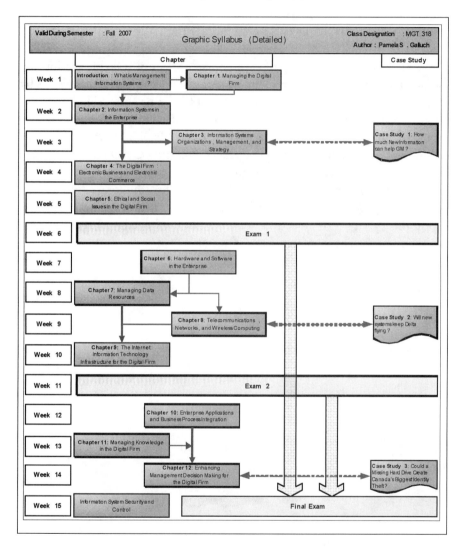

Sport Management for Intercollegiate Athletics

Leslie Moreland created the eye-catching graphic syllabus in Figure A.22 for her course, Sport Management for Intercollegiate Athletics. As do Dr. Coffee's graphic syllabus for Culinary Techniques (Figure 3.12) and Dr. Smith's for Systems Programming Concepts for Computer Engineering (Figure A.9), Ms. Moreland's syllabus winds its way down the page in alternating directions. She is able to make the beginning of each course unit unmistakably obvious by framing the unit's key question in an explosion-shaped enclosure, as well as by changing the color of the unit's enclosures. The exams and assignments due are also clearly highlighted outside of the enclosures in another typeface. Ms. Moreland phrased each topic as a question, as did Ms. Walker and Dr. Campbell in their graphic syllabi for Managerial Accounting Concepts (Figure A.2) and Small Business Management (Figure A.14), respectively.

The outcomes map that Ms. Moreland made for this course (Figure 4.5) looks nothing like her graphic syllabus. The former shows students progressing up through a list of objectives and does not (and need not) reveal the organization of the course material into three units.

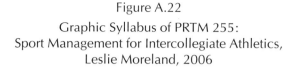

Figure A.22
Graphic Syllabus of PRTM 255:
Sport Management for Intercollegiate Athletics,
Leslie Moreland, 2006

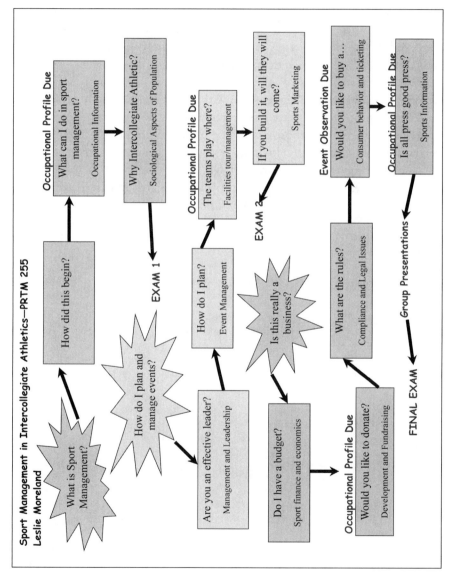

E-Commerce and Tourism Marketing

Figure A.23 displays Irem Arsal's graphic syllabus of her E-Commerce and Tourism Marketing course. It moves from top to bottom. It also moves outward from the center and back again when distinguishing categories such as demand- versus supply-driven e-tourism and the different industry sectors. This gives it a look distinct from the other graphic syllabi previously showcased. While simple and crisp, it notates the chapter assignments, the four exams, and the chapters each exam covers.

What is not evident in the black-and-white reproduction is Ms. Arsal's smart use of color to match up content with exams—that is, all the enclosures that frame topics covered in the first exam are one color, the same color as the Exam 1 enclosure; all of those that frame topics covered in the second exam are another color, the same color as the Exam 2 enclosure, and so on.

In her outcomes map (Figure 4.6), Ms. Arsal chose only one color for all the enclosures. It, too, is simple and crisp and has a similar look, except that it moves from left to right, then top to bottom.

Figure A.23

Graphic Syllabus of PRTM 391: E-Commerce and Tourism Marketing, Irem Arsal, 2006

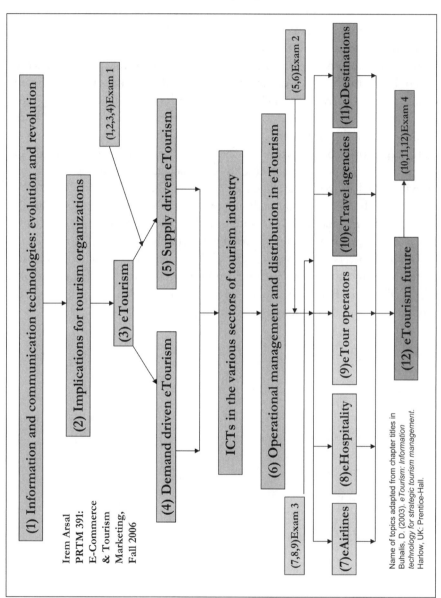

Introductory Psychology

Now a Professor of Curriculum and Instruction at the University of Victoria in British Columbia, Canada, Dr. Martin Wall was professor of psychology at the University of Toronto when he designed his graphic syllabus for Introductory Psychology in Figure A.24. Overall the graphic moves from top to bottom, but it also shifts to the left, to the right, and out from the center to represent the variety of relationships among the major topics. It can encompass only the major topics on one page because this introductory psychology course spans two terms. The fall term opens with the study of psychology and proceeds into the many facets of brain-based behavior: motivation and learning, then mental processes such as perception, memory, thinking, and language. Any in-depth treatment of research methods is put off until the beginning of the spring term and followed by social factors, development, and individual differences in intelligence and personality, all of which impact the presence or absence of psychopathology, which closes the course. Dr. Wall also inserted the term tests and final exam into the syllabus. What is not evident in Figure A.24 is his use of color to group more closely related topics together.

At the University of Toronto, Dr. Wall also taught a graduate-level course on teaching psychology in which he had his students try their hand at graphic syllabi. The three figures that follow Figure A.24 are just a few of his students' products and should be viewed as works in progress.

Figure A.24
Graphic Syllabus of PSY 100: Introductory Psychology,
Dr. Martin Wall, 2005

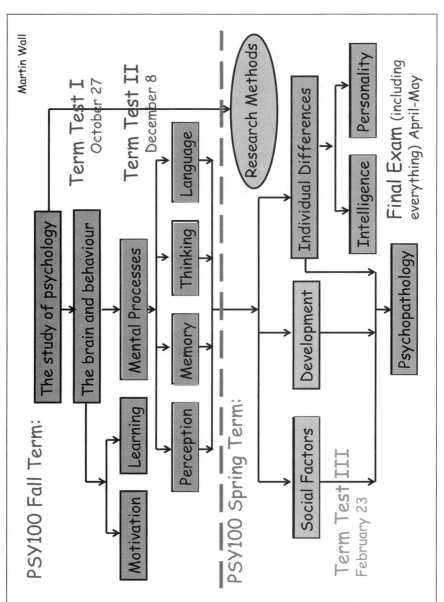

Social Development

One of Dr. Wall's graduate students, Alisa Almas, composed a graphic syllabus for her summer school psychology course, Social Development (see Figure A.25). She included the textbook's chapter numbers, making it easier to follow the flow of topics.

After the introduction, the course addresses classic theories of social development, then contemporary theories, and moves on to topics related to the development of the self: temperament, attachment relationships, the self and social cognition, and sex/gender differences. The latter two topics lead into achievement, followed by aggression and antisocial conduct, and then altruism and moral development. At that point the focus shifts from the self to others: the family, other social contexts, and peer relations (including bullying). The course ends with a synthesis of the major topics.

Like her professor, Ms. Almas grouped related topics by color, which made her graphic syllabus more eye-catching and instructive.

Figure A.25
Graphic Syllabus of PSY 311: Social Development,
Alisa Almas, 2006

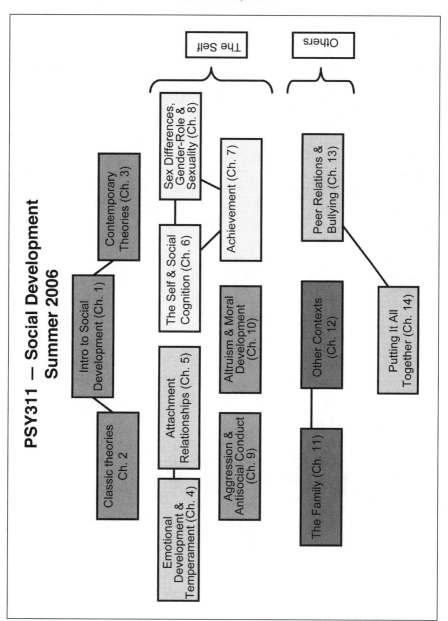

Psychology of Interpersonal Relationships

Tullia Leone, another one of Dr. Wall's graduate students, created her graphic syllabus for her course, Psychology of Interpersonal Relationships (see Figure A.26). The syllabus bears a coincidental resemblance to the one that Ms. Arsal designed for her E-Commerce and Tourism Marketing course (Figure A.23) in that its predominant direction is from top to bottom. It also moves outward from the center when it breaks down a major topic such as "Later Relationships: Initiation & Development" into subtopics ("Relationship Varieties," "Attraction," and "Maintenance"). Conversely, it moves back inward when subtopics such as "Cognitive Processes" and "Affective Processes" merge into the larger topics of "Love & Sex" and "Dissolution and Loss."

Ms. Leona enhanced the eye appeal and instructional value of her graphic syllabus by identifying similar and complementary topics by color. In her original version, "First Relationships..." and "Later Relationships..." are both in pink enclosures. "Relationship Varieties," "Attraction," and "Maintenance" are in blue enclosures, "Cognitive Processes" and "Affective Processes" are in gray, "Love & Sex" and "Dissolution and Loss" are in purple, and "Mental Health" and "Physical Health" are in yellow.

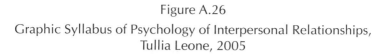

Figure A.26
Graphic Syllabus of Psychology of Interpersonal Relationships,
Tullia Leone, 2005

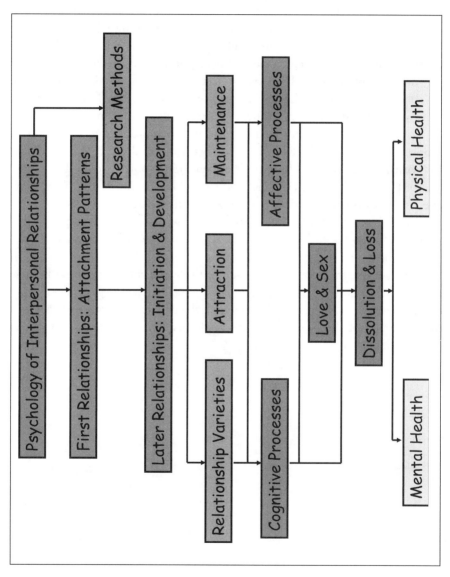

Psychology of Perception

While each is different in its own right, the last two graphic syllabi each have a flowchart design. The one that Christine Burton composed for *Psychology of Perception* (see Figure A.27) breaks different ground. She arranged her course topics within a double oval, a variation on a "circle map," which Hyerle (1996) developed to show context. The outermost oval, which is where the course begins, places the entire field of perception in the historical context of why and how we study it. The adjacent oval provides another layer of context or "common ground" for the course topics within; they all are facets of perceptual awareness and attention. Inside both large ovals are four smaller ovals, one for each perceptual system: the visual, the auditory, proprioception (the perception of stimuli produced inside the organism), and the chemical senses. The visual system involves four kinds of perception (object, color, depth, and motion); the auditory system, one kind (sound localization); proprioception, one kind (touch); and the chemical sense, two kinds (smell and taste).

Ms. Burton reinforced her spatial design with color. The context ovals are dark blue and light blue, and each of the four "sense" ovals is a different warm color.

To serve students in a course most effectively, the graphic needs additional order and flow among the ovals. The two context topics suggest material for the first few weeks, but the order in which the course addresses each perceptual system is not clear. The sense ovals might benefit from greater internal detail as well.

Figure A.27
Graphic Syllabus of Psychology of Perception,
Christine Burton, 2005

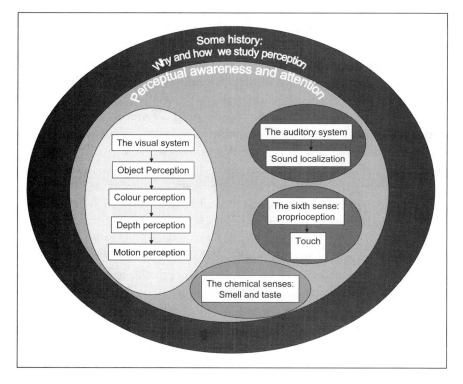

Metabolic and Molecular Basis of Medicine

Figure A.28 shows another distinctive graphic syllabus, this one designed by Dr. Donald Gillian-Daniel, assistant director of the Delta Program in Research, Teaching, and Learning in the Delta Internship Program at the University of Wisconsin–Madison. Dr. Gillian-Daniel also teaches in the university's Department of Comparative Biosciences at the School of Veterinary Medicine. His graphic syllabus is for the six-week professional course, Metabolic and Molecular Basis of Medicine, an intensive four-credit requirement in the veterinary medicine program.

As shown in the graphic, carbohydrate metabolism receives the first two weeks of attention and includes the topic of redox reactions, which are involved in catabolism. Protein metabolism is covered in the first part of the third week, and lipid metabolism in the rest of the third week and the entire fourth week. The metabolic interrelationships among all of these biochemical processes is taught in the fifth week, followed by the exam. For each topic, the syllabus provides the relevant page numbers for the study guide.

Without being cluttered, Dr. Gillian-Daniel's graphic syllabus contains considerable content. It presents simplified diagrams of catabolism (the breakdown of complex substances into simpler, small units to release energy) and anabolism (the synthesis or combination of simpler substances into more complex ones, which requires energy) for carbohydrates, lipids, and proteins. These thumbnail drawings help students distill the essential differences and similarities among the metabolic processes for each type of molecule.

Figure A.28

Graphic Syllabus of #934–502:
Metabolic and Molecular Basis of Medicine,
Dr. Donald Gillian-Daniel, 2007

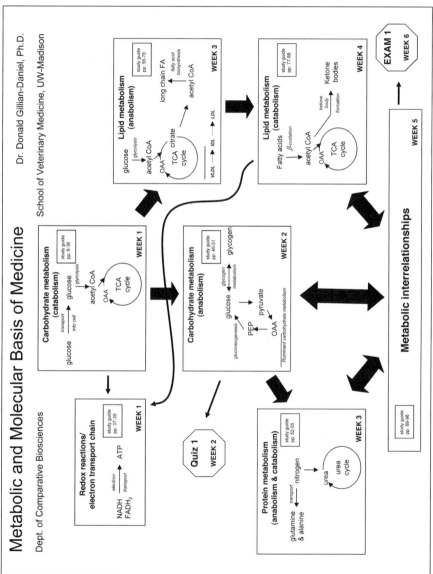

Computer Software for Graphic Syllabi and Outcomes Maps

Most of the graphic syllabi and outcomes maps in this book were prepared in Microsoft Word or PowerPoint using the Drawing, Visual Basic, and/or Word Art tools. In addition, one was produced in Microsoft Excel, one in Microsoft Publisher, and one in AutoCAD.

Although many people have Microsoft software products on their computers, some find them unwieldy for generating graphics. Fortunately, affordable alternatives are available. Table B.1 provides basic information obtained from company web sites (in January 2007) on commercial software that was developed specifically for creating graphics electronically. A considerable variety of programs are on the market at reasonable prices, and all but two companies, Inspiration Software, Inc. and Mind Technologies AS, give educational discounts. (Inspiration's products are designed for educators and are priced accordingly.) All of the companies offer quantity discounts and network licensing packages to make department- and college-wide purchases more affordable. In addition, the companies invite potential buyers to download a free trial version so that they can experiment with the software for a period of time.

Even a novice user of graphics software can quickly become proficient in the basics of these programs. They all come with preinstalled tutorials, sample graphics, and templates. Instructors can use varied fonts, styles, colors, patterns, and shapes to design flowcharts, diagrams, and other graphics. They can also access vast collections of symbols and import images in different formats to visually communicate and/or highlight certain ideas.

Some of the programs can even incorporate sound files, permitting instructors to add a talking interface to their graphics. This feature is particularly useful in distance education courses and, even in the traditional classroom, facilitates the learning of auditory and visually challenged learners.

All the software options can export finished graphics onto web pages as well as incorporate hyperlinks, allowing students easy access to web-based resources for learning and research. The export capabilities enable users to save a graphic in different formats and to send it to others to view and print, regardless of whether they have the software in which it was created. With the Windows version, users can easily export visuals into other Microsoft programs, such as Word, PowerPoint, Project, and Outlook. Many companies provide different export options as well as free, downloadable viewer programs that enable users without the full software package to open, view, and print the graphics.

All of the programs work with the Windows operating system. Concept-Draw, MindMapper, and Inspiration have Macintosh versions as well. Several companies sell special versions of their software for Tablet PCs (e.g., MindGenius and MindManager) and for handheld computers (e.g., MindManager and MindMapper). Some of the programs are available in languages other than English.

For the latest information on software versions, features, options, and prices, call the companies or go to their web sites. Contact information is provided in Table B.1.

Table B.1

Information on Computer Software for Graphic Syllabi
and Outcomes Maps

Product	Price, Education Discount	Operating System(s)	Company Information	
			Name	Telephone Web Site
ConceptDraw MINDMAP 4	$99 Yes	Windows Macintosh	Computer Systems Odessa, LCC	1-877-441-1150 www.conceptdraw.com
EDGE Diagrammer	$59.95 Yes	Windows	Pacestar Software	1-480-893-3046 www.pacestar.com
Inspiration 8	$69 No	Windows Macintosh	Inspiration Software, Inc.	1-800-877-4292 www.inspiration.com
MindGenius Education V2	$107 Yes	Windows	Gael Ltd.	+44 (0) 355-247766 www.mindgenius.com
MindManager Basic 6, Pro 6	$115, $149 Yes	Windows	Mindjet	1-877-646-3538 www.mindjet.com
MindMapper Professional 5	$179.95 Yes	Windows Macintosh	SimTech Systems, Inc.	1-972-436-0863 or 1-877-883-6505 www.mindmapperusa .com/products.htm
VisiMap Professional 4	£19 Yes	Windows	CoCo Systems Ltd.	+44 7971-321586 or 1-800-884-0489 (orders) www.coco.co.uk
Visual Mind 8 Basic, Business	$99, $149 No	Windows	Mind Technologies AS	+47 3285 5455 www.visual-mind.com

Bibliography

Alexander, P. A. (1996). The past, the present, and the future of knowledge research: A reexamination of the role of knowledge in learning and instruction. *Educational Psychologist, 31*(2), 89–92.

Anderson, J. R. (1993, January). Problem solving and learning. *American Psychologist, 48*(1), 35–44.

Anderson, L. W., & Krathwohl, D. R. (Eds.). (2000). *A taxonomy for learning, teaching, and assessing: A revision of Bloom's taxonomy of educational objectives.* New York, NY: Allyn & Bacon.

Anderson, R. C. (1984, November). Some reflection on the acquisition of knowledge. *Educational Researcher, 13*(9), 5–10.

Angelo, T. A., & Cross, K. P. (1993). *Classroom assessment techniques: A handbook for college teachers* (2nd ed.). San Francisco, CA: Jossey-Bass.

Ausubel, D. P. (1968). *Educational psychology: A cognitive view.* New York, NY: Holt, Rinehart, & Winston.

Avgerinou, M., & Ericson, J. (1997, October). A review of the concept of visual literacy. *British Journal of Educational Technology, 28*(4), 280–291.

Baugh, N. G., & Mellot, K. G. (1998, September). Clinical concept mapping as preparation for student nurses' clinical experiences. *Journal of Nursing Education, 37*(6), 253–256.

Baxter Magolda, M. B. (1992). *Knowing and reasoning in college: Gender-related patterns in students' intellectual development.* San Francisco, CA: Jossey-Bass.

Beissner, K. L. (1992, Spring). Use of concept mapping to improve problem solving. *Journal of Physical Therapy, 6*(1), 22–27.

Biktimirov, E. N., & Nilson, L. B. (2003, July/August). Mapping your course: Designing a graphic syllabus for introductory finance. *Journal of Education for Business, 78*(6), 308–312.

Biktimirov, E. N., & Nilson, L. B. (2006, Fall). Show them the money: Using mind mapping in the introductory finance course. *Journal of Financial Education, 32,* 72–86.

Biktimirov, E. N., & Nilson, L. B. (2007, Summer). Adding animation and interactivity to finance courses with learning objects. *Journal of Financial Education, 33,* 35–47.

Bligh, D. A. (2000). *What's the use of lectures?* San Francisco, CA: Jossey-Bass.

Bloom, B. S. (Ed.). (1956). *Taxonomy of educational objectives, handbook 1: Cognitive domain.* New York, NY: Longman.

Blue, T. (2002). *I don't know* how *to read this book!* Retrieved June 7, 2007, from www.teacherblue.homestead.com/cantread.html

Bonwell, C. C., & Eison, J. A. (1991). *Active learning: Creating excitement in the classroom* (ASHE-ERIC Higher Education Report No. 1). Washington, DC: The George Washington University, School of Education and Human Development.

Boyer, E. L. (1990). *Scholarship reconsidered: Priorities of the professoriate.* Princeton, NJ: The Carnegie Foundation for the Advancement of Teaching.

Bransford, J. D., Brown, A. L., & Cocking, R. R. (Eds.). (1999). *How people learn: Brain, mind, experience, and school.* Washington, DC: National Academy Press.

Brinkmann, A. (2003, February). Mind mapping as a tool in mathematics education. *Mathematics Teacher, 96*(2), 96–101.

Briscoe, C., & LaMaster, S. U. (1991, April). Meaningful learning in college biology through concept mapping. *American Biology Teacher, 53*(4), 214–219.

Burchfield, C. M., & Sappinton, J. (2000, Winter). Compliance with required reading assignments. *Teaching of Psychology, 27*(1), 58–60.

Buzan, T. (1974). *Use your head.* London, UK: BBC Books.

Buzan, T. (1991). *Use both sides of your brain* (3rd ed.). New York, NY: Plume.

Carey, S. (1985). Are children fundamentally different kinds of thinkers and learners than adults? In S. F. Chipman, J. W. Segal, & R. Glaser (Eds.), *Thinking and learning skills: Research and open questions* (Vol. 2, pp. 485–517). Hillsdale, NJ: Lawrence Erlbaum Associates.

Carlile, O., & Jordan, A. (2005). It works in practice but will it work in theory? The theoretical underpinnings of pedagogy. In G. O'Neill, S. Moore, & B. McMullin (Eds.), *Emerging issues in the practice of university teaching* (pp. 11–25). Dublin, Ireland: All Ireland Society for Higher Education.

Chi, M. T. H., Glaser, R., & Rees, E. (1982). Expertise in problem solving. In R. Sternberg (Ed.), *Advances in the psychology of human intelligence* (Vol. 4, pp. 7–75). Hillsdale, NJ: Lawrence Erlbaum Associates.

Clark, J. M., & Paivio, A. (1991). Dual coding theory and education. *Educational Psychology Review, 3*(3), 149–210.

Cliburn, J. W., Jr. (1990, February). Concepts to promote meaningful learning. *Journal of College Science Teaching, 19*(4), 212–217.

Crouch, C. H., & Mazur, E. (2001, September). Peer instruction: Ten years of experience and results. *American Journal of Physics, 69*(9), 970–977.

Cyrs, T. E. (1997). *Teaching at a distance with the merging technologies: An instructional systems approach.* Las Cruces, NM: New Mexico State University, Center for Educational Development.

de Jong, T., & Ferguson-Hessler, M. G. M. (1996). Types and quality of knowledge. *Educational Psychologist, 31*(2), 105–113.

Driver, M. (2001, September/October). Fostering creativity in business education: Developing creative classroom environments to provide students with critical workplace competencies. *Journal of Education for Business, 77*(1), 28–33.

Ellis, D. (2000). *Becoming a master student* (9th ed.). Boston, MA: Houghton Mifflin.

Eriksson, L. T., & Hauer, A. M. (2004, February). Mind map marketing: A creative approach in developing marketing skills. *Journal of Marketing Education, 26*(2), 174–187.

Eyler, J., & Giles, D. E., Jr. (1999). *Where's the learning in service-learning?* San Francisco, CA: Jossey-Bass.

Farrand, P., Hussain, F., & Hennessy, E. (2002, May). The efficacy of the "mind map" study technique. *Medical Education, 36*(5), 426–431.

Filbeck, G., & Smith, L. L. (1996, Spring/Summer). Learning styles, teaching strategies, and predictors of success for students in corporate finance. *Financial Practice and Education, 6*(1), 74–85.

Fink, L. D. (2003). *Creating significant learning experiences: An integrated approach to designing college courses.* San Francisco, CA: Jossey-Bass.

Fischman, G. E. (2001, November). Reflections about images, visual culture, and educational research. *Educational Researcher, 30*(8), 28–33.

Fleming, N. D., & Mills, C. (1992). Not another inventory, rather a catalyst for reflection. In D. H. Wulff & J. D. Nyquist (Eds.), *To improve the academy: Vol. 11. Resources for faculty, instructional, and organizational development* (pp. 137–149). Stillwater, OK: New Forums Press.

Gedalof, A. J. (1998). *Teaching large classes* (Green Guide No. 1). Halifax, NS: Society for Teaching and Learning in Higher Education.

Glaser, R. (1991). The maturing of the relationship between the science of learning and cognition and educational practice. *Learning and Instruction, 1*(2), 129–144.

Goodson, L. (2005, March). *Content, presentation and learning activities.* Paper presented at the annual meeting of the Southern Regional Faculty and Instructional Development Consortium, Lake Junaluska, NC.

Gray, M. J., Ondaatje, E. H., Fricker, R. D., Jr., & Geschwind, S. A. (2000, March/April). Assessing service-learning: Results from a survey of "Learn and Serve America, Higher Education." *Change, 32*(2), 30–39.

Grunert, J. (1997). *The course syllabus: A learning-centered approach.* Bolton, MA: Anker.

Hallett, V. (2005, July 25). The power of Potter: Can the teenage wizard turn a generation of halfhearted readers into lifelong bookworms? *U.S. News & World Report.* Retrieved June 7, 2007, from www.usnews.com/usnews/culture/articles/050725/25read.htm

Hartman, J. L. (2006, June). *Teaching and learning in the Net Generation.* Paper presented at the annual meeting of the Association of American University Presses, New Orleans, LA.

Hobson, E. H. (2004). *Getting students to read: Fourteen tips* (IDEA Paper No. 40). Manhattan, KS: Kansas State University, Center for Faculty Evaluation and Development.

Hodgins, H. W. (2000). *Into the future: A vision paper.* Retrieved June 7, 2007, from www.learnativity.com/download/MP7.PDF

Hoffman, E., Trott, J., & Neely, K. P. (2002, September). Concept mapping: A tool to bridge the disciplinary divide. *American Journal of Obstetrics and Gynecology, 187*(Suppl. 3), S41–S43.

Hyerle, D. (1996). *Visual tools for constructing knowledge.* Alexandria, VA: Association for Supervision and Curriculum Development.

Katayama, A. D. (1997, November). *Getting students involved in note taking: Why partial notes benefit learners more than complete notes.* Paper presented at the annual meeting of the Mid-South Educational Research Association, Memphis, TN.

Kinchin, I. M. (2000). Concept mapping in biology. *Journal of Biological Education, 34*(2), 61–68.

Kinchin, I. M. (2001, December). If concept mapping is so helpful to learning biology, why aren't we all using it? *International Journal of Science Education, 23*(12), 1257–1269.

King, M., & Shell, R. (2002, September–October). Teaching and evaluating critical thinking with concept maps. *Nurse Educator, 27*(5), 214–216.

Kosslyn, S. M. (1994). *Image and brain: The resolution of the imagery debate.* Cambridge, MA: MIT Press.

Kozma, R. B., Russell, J., Jones, T., Marx, N., & Davis, J. (1996). The use of multiple, linked representations to facilitate science understanding. In S. Vosniadou, E. De Corte, R. Glaser, & H. Mandl (Eds.), *International perspectives on the design of technology-supported learning environments* (pp. 41–60). Mahwah, NJ: Lawrence Erlbaum Associates.

Kuhn, T. S. (1970). *The structure of scientific revolutions* (2nd ed.). Chicago, IL: University of Chicago Press.

Larkin, J. H., & Simon, H. A. (1987). Why a diagram is (sometimes) worth ten thousand words. *Cognitive Science, 11*(1), 65–99.

Leamnson, R. (2000, November/December). Learning as biological brain change. *Change, 32*(6), 34–40.

Leauby, B. A., & Brazina, P. (1998, Winter). Concept mapping: Potential uses in accounting education. *Journal of Accounting Education, 16*(1), 123–138.

Leichhardt, G. (1989). Development of an expert explanation: An analysis of a sequence of subtraction lessons. In L. Resnick (Ed.), *Knowing, learning, and instruction* (pp. 67–125). Hillsdale, NJ: Lawrence Erlbaum Associates.

Mangurian, L. P. (2005, November). *Learning and teaching practice: The power of the affective.* Paper presented at the 25th annual Lilly Conference on College Teaching, Oxford, OH.

Marshall, P. (1974, November). How much, how often? *College and Research Libraries, 35*(6), 453–456.

Mayer, R. E., & Gallini, J. K. (1990, December). When is an illustration worth ten thousand words? *Journal of Educational Psychology, 82*(4), 715–726.

Mayer, R. E., & Sims, V. K. (1994, September). For whom is a picture worth ten thousand words? Extensions of a dual coding theory of multimedia learning. *Journal of Educational Psychology, 86*(3), 389–401.

McClain, A. (1987, Summer). Improving lectures: Challenging both sides of the brain. *Journal of Optometric Education, 13*(1), 18–20.

McDougall, D., & Cordiero, P. (1993, January–March). Effects of random-questioning expectations on community college students' preparedness for lecture and discussion. *Community College Journal of Research and Practice, 17*(1), 39–49.

McGaghie, W. C., McCrimmon, D. R., Mitchell, G., Thompson, J. A., & Ravitch, M. M. (2000, June). Quantitative concept mapping in pulmonary physiology: Comparison of student and faculty knowledge structures. *Advances in Physiology Education, 23*(1), 72–81.

Mealy, D. L., & Nist, S. L. (1989). Postsecondary teacher directed comprehension strategies. *Journal of Reading, 32*(6), 484–493.

Mento, A. J., Martinelli, P., & Jones, R. M. (1999). Mind mapping in executive education: Applications and outcomes. *Journal of Management Development, 18*(4), 390–407.

Moreno, R., & Mayer, R. E. (1999, June). Cognitive principles of multimedia learning: The role of modality and contiguity. *Journal of Educational Psychology, 91*(2), 358–368.

Nathan, R. (2005). *My freshman year: What a professor learned by becoming a student.* Ithaca, NY: Cornell University Press.

Nettleship, J. (1992, Summer). Active learning in economics: Mind maps and wall charts. *Economics, 28*(118), 69–71.

Nilson, L. B. (2003). *Teaching at its best: A research-based resource for college instructors* (2nd ed.). Bolton, MA: Anker.

Nixon-Cobb, E. (2005, February). Visualizing thinking: A strategy that improves thinking. *The Teaching Professor, 19*(2), 3, 6.

Novak, J. D. (1977). An alternative to Piagetian psychology for sciences and mathematics education. *Science Education, 61*(4), 453–477.

Paivio, A. (1971). *Imagery and verbal processes.* New York, NY: Holt, Rinehart, & Winston.

Paivio, A. (1990). *Mental representations: A dual coding approach.* New York, NY: Oxford University Press.

Paivio, A., & Csapo, K. (1973). Picture superiority in free recall: Imagery and dual coding? *Cognitive Psychology, 5,* 176–206.

Paivio, A., Walsh, M., & Bons, T. (1994). Concreteness effects on memory: When and why? *Journal of Experimental Psychology: Learning, Memory, and Cognition, 20*(5), 1196–1204.

Perry, W. G., Jr. (1968). *Forms of educational and ethical development in the college years: A scheme.* New York, NY: Holt, Rinehart, & Winston.

Plotnick, E. (2001). A graphical system for understanding the relationship between concepts. *Teacher Librarian, 28*(4), 42–44.

Prégent, R. (1994). *Charting your course: How to prepare to teach more effectively.* Madison, WI: Atwood.

Rebich, S., & Gautier, C. (2005, September). Concept mapping to reveal prior knowledge and conceptual change in a mock summit course on global climate change. *Journal of Geoscience Education, 53*(4), 355–365.

Regis, A., & Albertazzi, P. G. (1996, November). Concept maps in chemistry education. *Journal of Chemical Education, 73*(11), 1084–1088.

Reif, F., & Heller, J. I. (1982). Knowledge structure and problem solving in physics. *Educational Psychologist, 17*(2), 102–127.

Rhem, J. (1995, December). Close up: Going deep. *The National Teaching and Learning Forum, 5*(1), 4.

Robinson, D. H., Katayama, A. D., DuBois, N. F., & Devaney, T. (1998, Fall). Interactive effects of graphic organizers and delayed review of concept application. *Journal of Experimental Education, 67*(1), 17–31.

Robinson, D. H., & Kiewra, K. A. (1995, September). Visual argument: Graphic organizers are superior to outlines in improving learning from text. *Journal of Educational Psychology, 87*(3), 455–467.

Robinson, D. H., & Molina, E. (2002, January). The relative involvement of visual and auditory working memory when studying adjunct displays. *Contemporary Educational Psychology, 27*(1), 118–131.

Robinson, D. H., & Schraw, G. (1994, October). Computational efficiency through visual argument: Do graphic organizers communicate relations in text too effectively? *Contemporary Educational Psychology, 19*(4), 399–414.

Robinson, D. H., & Skinner, C. H. (1996, April). Why graphic organizers facilitate search processes: Fewer words or computationally efficient indexing? *Contemporary Educational Psychology, 21*(2), 166–180.

Romance, N. R., & Vitale, M. R. (1997). *Knowledge representation systems: Basis for the design of instruction for undergraduate course curriculum.* Paper presented at the 8th annual National Conference on College Teaching and Learning, Jacksonville, FL.

Romance, N. R., & Vitale, M. R. (1999, Spring). Concept mapping as a tool for learning: Broadening the framework for student-centered instruction. *College Teaching, 47*(2), 74–79.

Rowe, M. B. (1980). Pausing principles and their effects on reasoning in science. In F. B. Brawer (Ed.), *New directions for community colleges: No. 31. Teaching the sciences* (pp. 27–34). San Francisco, CA: Jossey-Bass.

Royer, J. M., Cisero, C. A., & Carlo, M. S. (1993, Summer). Techniques and procedures for assessing cognitive skills. *Review of Educational Research, 63*(2), 201–243.

Ruhl, K. L., Hughes, C. A., & Schloss, P. J. (1987, Winter). Using the pause procedure to enhance lecture recall. *Teacher Education and Special Education, 10*(1), 14–18.

Schau, C., & Mattern, N. (1997, May). Use of map techniques in teaching applied statistics courses. *American Statistician, 51*(2), 171–175.

Schuster, P. M. (2000). Concept mapping: Reducing clinical care plan paperwork and increasing learning. *Nurse Educator, 25* (2), 76–81.

Self, J. (1987). Reserve reading and student grades: Analysis of a case study. *Library and Information Science Research, 9*(1), 29–40.

Sirias, D. (2002, September). Using graphic organizers to improve the teaching of business statistics. *Journal of Education for Business, 78*(1), 33–37.

Soleil, L. S. (2003, February 26). Summary of responses: Reading assignment quantity guidelines. Message posted to the POD Network electronic mailing list, archived at http://listserv.nd.edu/cgi-bin/wa?A2=ind0302 &L=pod&F=&S=&P=20435

Svinicki, M. D. (2004). *Learning and motivation in the postsecondary classroom.* Bolton, MA: Anker.

Theall, M. (1997, May). *Overview of different approaches to teaching and learning styles.* Paper presented at the Central Illinois Higher Education Consortium Faculty Development Conference, Springfield, IL.

Tigner, R. B. (1999, September). Putting memory research to good use: Hints from cognitive psychology. *College Teaching, 47*(1), 149–152.

Tversky, B. (1995). Cognitive origins of conventions. In F. T. Marchese (Ed.), *Understanding images: Finding meaning in digital imagery* (pp. 29–53). New York, NY: Springer-Verlag.

Tversky, B. (2001). Spatial schemas in depictions. In M. Gattis (Ed.), *Spatial schemas and abstract thought* (pp. 79–111). Cambridge, MA: MIT Press.

Vekiri, I. (2002, September). What is the value of graphical displays in learning? *Educational Psychology Review, 14*(3), 261–312.

Vojtek, B., & Vojtek, R. (2000, Fall). Technology: Visual learning—This software helps organize ideas and concepts. *Journal of Staff Development, 21*(4). Retrieved June 7, 2007, from www.nsdc.org/library/publications/jsd/vojtek 214.cfm

Wallace, J. D., & Mintzes, J. J. (1990, December). The concept map as a research tool: Exploring conceptual change in biology. *Journal of Research in Science Teaching, 27*(10), 1033–1052.

Waller, R. (1981, April). *Understanding network diagrams.* Paper presented at the annual meeting of the American Educational Research Association, Los Angeles, CA.

Weber, M. (1930). *The Protestant ethic and the spirit of capitalism.* London, UK: Allen & Unwin.

West, D. C., Pomeroy, J. R., Park, J. K., Gerstenberger, E. A., & Sandoval, J. (2000, September). Critical thinking in graduate medical education: A role for concept mapping assessment? *Journal of the American Medical Association, 284*(9), 1105–1110.

Wilkes, L., Cooper, K., Lewin, J., & Batts, J. (1999, January/February). Concept mapping: Promoting science learning in BN learners in Australia. *Journal of Continuing Education in Nursing, 30*(1), 37–44.

Winn, W. (1987). Charts, graphs, and diagrams in educational materials. In D. M. Willows & H. A. Houghton (Eds.), *The psychology of illustration: Basic research* (Vol. 1, pp. 152–198). New York, NY: Springer-Verlag.

Winn, W. (1991, September). Learning from maps and diagrams. *Educational Psychology Review, 3*(3), 211–247.

Wycoff, J. (1991). *Mindmapping: Your personal guide to exploring creativity and problem-solving.* New York, NY: Berkley Books.

Zeilik, M., Schau, C., Mattern, N., Hall, S., Teague, K. W., & Bisard, W. (1997, October). Conceptual astronomy: A novel model for teaching postsecondary science courses. *American Journal of Physics, 65*(10), 987–996.

Index